From the South Pacific to The New River

A West Virginia Love Story

John Emerson Campbell

John Emerson Campbell

ISBN: 978-1-916770-04-1

Dedications

To all of our Servicemen who have and are currently representing and keeping our country safe.

Prelude: From the South Pacific to the New River

This story is about our father John Emerson Campbell who was a Navy Mid-Shipman during WWII and Delphia Mae Wininger Campbell, our mother.

We have letters written by our father to our mother starting on March 27, 1944, through September 7, 1945.

This is a love story of letters that became a couple who married and raised three children.

It is written with respect, gratitude, and remembrance of them and also of others whose stories were and are somewhat similar.

Table Of Contents

Dedications	iii
Prelude: From the South Pacific to the New River	iv
Herbert's Death Certificate	viii
March 27, 1944	1
April 18, 1944	4
June 3, 1944	7
June 30, 1944	9
July 28, 1944	11
August 14, 1944	13
August 24, 1944	15
Sept 10, 1944	18
John Campbell in Uniform	20
Del Wininger at the age of 16	21
Sept. 26, 1944	22
Del with Dog	25
Oct. 10, 1944	26
Oct. 22, 1944	28
Nov. 1, 1944	30
Nov. 15, 1944	33
Nov. 27, 1944	35
Dec. 7, 1944	40
Dec. 12, 1944	43
Dec. 23, 1944	46

Jan. 3, 1945   48

Jan. 10, 1945   51

Jan. 27, 1945   54

Feb. 1, 1945   57

Feb. 6, 1945   59

Feb. 15, 1945   61

March 4, 1945   63

March 6, 1945   66

March 16, 1945   68

March 22, 1945   71

March 29, 1945   74

April 2, 1945   77

April 11, 1945   79

April 20, 1945   83

May 1, 1945   90

May 7, 1945   92

May 18, 1945   95

May 20, 1945   97

May 22, 1945   98

USS Taussig   100

New River Picture   101

May 30, 1945   102

June 5, 1945   105

June 10, 1945   109

June 16, 1945   113

June 19, 1945   117

June 27, 1945   120

July 6, 1945   123

July 10, 1945   126

July 16, 1945   129

July 21, 1945   132

July 29, 1945   136

August 5, 1945   138

August 16, 1945   144

August 18, 1945   147

Sept. 7, 1945   149

John Campbell's Service Statement   152

Marriage Certificate   157

From the South Pacific to the New River family members   159

Letter of Acknowledgement   162

Herbert's Death Certificate

In reply address not the signer of this
letter, but Bureau of Naval Personnel,
Navy Department, Washington, D. C.
Refer to No.

NAVY DEPARTMENT
BUREAU OF NAVAL PERSONNEL
WASHINGTON 25, D. C.

22 JAN 1944

P-5352 —n—jmn

From: Chief of Naval Personnel.
To: Addressee indicated.

Subject: CAMPBELL, Joseph Herbert, AMM2c, USNR, V-6, 552 74 23
Recalled to active duty 16 April 1942

Report of death of

Married No   Born Landisburg, W. Va.   Date 12 April 1922

Enlisted NRS, Charleston, W. Va.

Date 31 March 1942   Prior service None

Place of death NAS, Navy No. Thirty (Pacific area)

Date of death 22 December 1943 Attached to Carrier Aircraft Service Unit #4 (S&FS Dut

Nature of death Injuries, Multiple, Extreme – Struck by Airplane propeller

Death held NOT MISCONDUCT

Base Pay $96.00
Act 6/16/42   19.20
$115.20

NAME AND ADDRESS OF NEXT OF KIN

William Lee Campbell   Father   Landisburg, W. Va.
(Name)   (Relationship)   (Address)

PERSONS NAMED AS BENEFICIARIES

(Name)   (Relationship)   (Address)

RANDALL JACOBS
Chief of Naval Personnel

A. C. Jacobs
By direction

Addressee:
Bupers Statistics
Bu S & A (A. E. Div, -2)
Bu M & S (2)
Bu S & A (Allot. Div.)

Navy Relief Society
Vets. Ad. (2)
General Accounting Office

NAVPERS-1820

File copy

March 27, 1944

Hello Delphia,

I suppose you will be surprised that I should be writing you this letter. I should have talked to you some instead of writing, but there are a few things I want to tell you because I think you should know.

I am sure you knew Herbert thought a lot of you. In his own words, he said you were the girl he loved. I am sure he never changed his mind, but because of some people at home the two of you must have fallen out. He was some different from the average boy of his age and I am sure the Navy hadn't changed him much. People wrote him a letter and told him things that weren't true. Young men hear the older ones talk and they believe this. I guess it hurt him and he was a very stubborn fellow. How much you quarreled; I don't know. What was the reason I think I do? I want to say this to you and hope you understand my folks are deeply hurt. Ken is much more upset than people suspect. I am sure they like you, and I don't believe they said one word to him against you. I don't doubt, but what he told me things the others don't know. I think you were the only girl he ever cared for. You were the one person he wanted to come back to. Herb wasn't much on expressing himself in letters but I know I am not mistaken. Therefore, I want you to know he never changed his mind or feelings about you.

I would like to spare your feelings as much as possible but maybe I can best explain these things to you. He was killed in an accident at Maui. He was buried with full military honors there and I know the island where he was stationed. It is a very beautiful place. They were busy with invasion against Jap positions and although far from the action his work was winning for us. They will send his personal effects home and his body will be sent back after we have won. They will not leave sailors or marines buried out there. I do think you should know those things.

Delphia, you are a very young and sweet girl. I know this must have hurt you, and it has wrecked a lot of plans that I had. I have been around some, and it hurts to know he never got a chance to have any of the freedom he fought for. He realized as do the other boys that we must fight to help America for people like you. Every man out there knows the chance he must take, and they all know that some of them won't be back. To those boys who fell we owe something that can never be paid. It is only that they have not died in vain. Every one of them will be remembered and we won't let them down. It is our duty to see this through to victory for them and for the ones they love.

You will meet someone you love someday no doubt. You will be happy and I am sure he would want it that way. He was a star-spangled all-American kid who fought for victory in everything he went into. He knew the reason that he had to wear a uniform and I am proud today that he went without being called. Nothing can replace the respect I hold for him. Deep sorrow hangs over me now as I write this letter, but I am sure he would have done the same for me.

They will send his personal effects home. His shipmates say there are some pictures and I should think of other things that will be nice to keep. The folks lost his school ring after you gave it back. I don't know if he knew or not. If you would like to have something to keep, I will see you get it.

This letter has been hard to write. If there is anything you would like to know or any way I can help you I would be only glad to do so. It may be a long time before I get home again but I would like to see you then and talk to you some. War has entered the homes of many Americans. Sons and husbands have been killed and many more will go before it is over. Yet the young people who are only friends, or maybe they say sweethearts, get hurt too. The sorrow is the price we pay for victory. I am sure he was glad to be doing his part and you can be proud to say you were his friend. If you should care to write I would be only too glad to know you better. For now, I will say goodbye and the best of luck to you always.

Sincerely,

John

April 18, 1944

Hello Delphia,

I have been a little busy the past week and haven't had a chance to write you. I appreciate the letter you wrote and I think we understand each other much better now. I called my sister and told her you were to have anything you want that belonged to Herb. I doubt if you know her, but really, she is swell. If he had a navy ring or some symbol of his outfit, I would like you to have that. I will write Sister and tell her I am sure she will be more than glad to see you get it for he meant a lot to us all. Writing to you takes me into his personal life, and really, I didn't know him too well. I have been away from home for a long while. He wrote to me and through his letters I learned his attitude toward life. He was very loyal to his home and was glad to be able to fight for a country we all love. There is no doubt but that he was proud of the service he gave all for. I can just say this for him, Delphia. He has a respect set deep in me and no one can replace it. I am sure he was proud of me and I do not doubt that he chose the navy because of me. His feelings for you I cannot explain. I don't think I ever loved a girl as he did, but I do know how men feel out there. Please don't you regret what has happened? There is a grim reaper who will call us all and it was his hand that reached out to claim someone close to us. Although I am deeply hurt, I know he knew the score out there. Someone far greater than you or I is his master. That he was young hurts much worse we cannot forget, but we can console ourselves by saying he was doing his part in the fight to free the peace-loving people of the world. War is a terrible thing. It will change the lives of all who must fight for our country and it will hurt the folks left behind. Therefore, let you and I just say that he went in the service of a great cause and remember him as the fine young man that we both know he was. Please don't ever compare me with him. I cannot step on the same level, and I do not wish you to think I am his type.

I will not be in Norfolk much; I am going to school now and will go to a new destroyer in May. The U.S.S. Taussig DD#746. I guess we won't be around the States long and I doubt if I get home again, before we shove off. I would like to know you better and would appreciate letters from you. I am not so good at writing but I will do my best. If you would like to have things from foreign ports I will do my best to pick up some trinkets for you. A grass skirt would be nice if you want one. You can tell me in your next letter and I would be only too glad to do anything I can for you.

Delphia, you will always be more than welcome at my home. Mother and Dad are getting along in years, but they are swell. You could brighten up some day for them by a visit now and then. They are deeply hurt and they know how he felt about you. If I do get home, I want you to come down and have dinner with us. Your mother and dad also. It would be nice if we could all get together sometime and I'm sure, our folks would become friends.

I will be in New York a few weeks putting this ship in Commission. I have a lot of hard work ahead for she is a new type and the crew are young men. Most of them are just out of boot camp. They won't get too many older men and we will have to do more in our share. I want to be proud of this ship and I would like for her to make some hit at the enemy. It means a lot to me now.

This isn't much of a letter. I am putting in some long and hard days now so please excuse this one. I will try to make the ones in the future more interesting. So long for now and write to me sometime.

Sincerely,

John

P.S. These are the Campaign bars rating badge and gunner emblem he rated. I would like for you to keep them. The bars are for American defense, Pacific area and the naval reserve. The rating badge for AMM 2/C.

"Bye now"

John

June 3, 1944

Hello Delphia,

I guess you had begun to think I had forgotten you, but not in a million years. Just been a little busy and I am aboard ship again. A new one and is she a honey? I guess this one is about the newest type destroyer we have, and I am a lucky guy to get a ship like this.

I know you are enjoying the summer months at home after those long school days. I had much more fun on this last leave than ever before. I really thought you were swell and I appreciated talking with you. I can understand a lot of things now. We all have tragic incidents in life. The news just came in that our fifth army is in Rome. One step closer to Victory. It is great to know that we are winning and we can only hope it won't be long. Our boys will never let their pals down. They will go on and win for them for sure.

I have been having some fun since I was home. Got a chance to see some big-league baseball and I am crazy about the game. Most every year we hung around a radio and listened to the games. Now I have seen some of the guys I always wanted to see. Night games under lights and then a million other things to do. I have really enjoyed the past few weeks of my life. Just got a school paper a few days ago and I believe I know the - hand writing. Been a long time since I have seen the old dope sheet and it has changed a lot but I was glad to get it. I expect you miss some of the things that go with school days. Those people are the closest friends you will ever have. Most of my old classmates are gone now. The girls are married and the guys are in the armed forces. Many of them are over in Combat zones, but as far as I know not one of them hasn't so much as been wounded yet. *J.E. Campbell MM1/C* They were a swell bunch, and I only hope we can all have a nice home coming with all the other guys from the old school before long.

I guess everyone had comments to make about my girlfriend but it is nothing serious. Matter of fact I think I won't see her again. I like her and then I guess she just isn't my type. I don't want to get serious with any girl who doesn't think the same way I do. About some things I mean. She is a big city girl and I will never like city life. They are a nice place to visit but no place to stay. It is more like a big brother affair to her. More like you and I. Maybe she understands me, and she writes me letters to keep me going when I am away. Those letters help and I don't want you to forget. I won't write to often but I will expect answers.

If I should come home again this summer, I will be sure to see you again. Maybe if we can get some gas that we can go on a picnic or something. Down to Hawk's nest and the river. Take your kid brother. I like him. I think you will find I am not such a bad guy at times. I am going to call this finish for this time. Just got a call for some work. All I have been doing the past three days. Watches and work. Things will get better as the ship goes along. Just don't start breaking too many hearts up that way. Drop me a line when you have time and best of luck always.

Your friend,

John

J.E.Campbell MM1/C

June 30, 1944

Hello Delphia,

Got your most welcome letter, and I can't understand what made you think I would stop writing to you. I will be sending you these silly letters until sometime that you decide you don't want to write anymore. You give me news and other things I like to know about. Maybe you are my good luck charm. No one said you must wait until I answer your letter to write again. My mail goes through a censor and it is hard for me to think of things to write just any time. You can write anything you care to and I do enjoy your letters.

I suppose you do have a swell time there now that summer is in full swing. I think back over all the fun we once had on the farm. There isn't anything in my life to compare with those days. We were always fighting and I was always blamed for starting the trouble. I have never been home in the summer time since I came into the navy. With a little luck, I might make it this year. Sure, hope so anyway for I don't believe I was ever more homesick than I am now. I would like to see Dot. She has always been my pet, but I guess she will be going home soon. She has grown a lot since I have been away, but everyone has changed. I don't suppose you were living there when I was a civilian. Anyway, I don't remember you except once when I was home on leave.

Someone has the wrong idea when they think I will get married. I saw the girlfriend just once and the affair was over. She and I just don't see things alike so we just called it quits. I liked her but that was all. You sounded a bit enthused about who I would be with the next time I am home. Well, I don't know of any girls to date there anymore so I will probably be all by myself. Had a swell time after I came off leave. Saw some big *J.E. Campbell MM1/C* league baseball games and then there is a million things to do in a big city. Would like to take you out on a whirl sometime. I bet you would have the time of your life on the high-rides and side shows at some of those amusement parks. Then you would really get a thrill out of the floor shows at a nightclub. It is a lot of fun, but I will still come home every time I can.

I have some film for my camera now I just hope they are the correct size. Maybe I will use Sisters camera. I think the one I have lets air and light into the lens. Want to get some pictures of scenery if I can. Some nice places to get time shots at the state park and Hawks Nest. Got a million things to do if I get home. Tell Larry I would like to take him to go fishing with me. It is one of my favorite past times, but I never catch any fish. Maybe I will have some luck next time. When I was home all I did was break a new rod and almost cripple myself falling into the water. It was too cold to catch anything then.

They are sure moving along with this invasion in Europe. The way things are going now I guess maybe I will have to stay before my hair turns gray. It had me worried for a while though. Then I will have to look me up some girl for a wife. Probably won't have much luck though for all the young guys coming home will leave me on the sidelines. Can't blame a guy for trying and I never give up.

This is about all I can think up to write this time. Guess I had better secure now and get myself some much needed shut-eye. Don't forget to write. Bet you have a lot of fun on July 4th. Aof ll America has something to be proud of that day. Here wishing you a lot of fun this summer and "bye" now until the next time.

Always,

John

J.E. Campbell MM1/C

July 28, 1944

Dearest Delphia,

You sure weren't kidding when you promised to write and I appreciate your letter. It is a little different writing to you now than before. I had a very good time at home and rather hated to leave. I think I know you much better now and I like you a lot. You are much too young to get serious over anyone, and if you do you should pick someone of your age. You are and always will be a very dear friend. I would much rather it be that way. You would only get hurt by falling for me. I have been around too much and haven't lived the life that you have. I tried to tell you those things but you didn't listen to much. Better get that head of yours working and forget that you think I am a swell guy. I won't take advantage of you and try to make you care. Most guys would try to grab you off, but I only want you to be happy. Try going out with fellows. See if you don't feel different about me. Be sure of yourself and then maybe I will listen. It is just that you are so young and differ on opinions too much. I don't think it would work out so think it over.

I made good connections on the way back. A lucky break for me. Stopped by home again but just didn't have time to see you. Only had a few minutes at the train and some of the folks were down to see me off. I always hate to go and this time was the worse one of all. I wish you would have been there. Maybe I wouldn't have felt so bad then. You should go to camp and have fun with the rest. *J.E. Campbell MM 1/C*

I believe you think yourself grown up; you are still just a baby in my language so don't miss out on all the fun. People grow old fast. Live while you are young and live as young people do. Some of the pictures were swell. I guess I didn't hold the camera just right on others. Anyway, it was fun taking them. Sister sent me to the studio and had a picture made. If they turn out ok you can have one. If not, I will have another taken but really, I don't understand why you want a picture of this guy around. A baby must have it way though so I guess you get the picture.

I saw some of my old pals before I left. Home from the army and we had fun. They sure are a swell bunch of guys. Don't come any better and you can bet I want this war over so they can be home again. I guess I will get out also. Getting a little homesick again. Maybe seeing how people live just lets me know the things in life that I am missing. Maybe it won't be long now. This is a very bad excuse for a letter, but it is the best I can do now. I won't be writing to other girls there so don't worry your pretty head about what they say. They never had a chance with you around. Just write me any time you get time. I will appreciate all of your letters and even answer some of them. So, bye now and a nice time to you always.

As Ever,

John

J.E. Campbell MM 1/C

August 14, 1944

Hello Delphia,

I am a little surprised and plenty angry because you don't write. I have been waiting for a letter but not one word from you. Really, I didn't expect this letter writing to be a one-sided affair. You can write and you have much more time than I. Is it possible that something has happened and you don't care to answer my letters. You are and always will be my very best friend. I am sorry if I kid you some. You are just a baby as far as I'm concerned, and I wouldn't dare figure you any other way. I have been around and learned life the hard way. Things don't always work out as simple as they are planned. Any young girl as pretty and nice as you shouldn't have any trouble finding plenty of guys to date. Guys of your age and fellows who think the way you do. Much of my higher ideas on life have been destroyed, and a lot of trust in people is gone. I wouldn't dream of ever hurting you because of reasons you probably understand. I admire and respect you. Think of you as a wonderful friend and realize that the guy who steals your love will be a lucky guy. Letters don't come often enough for us to have arguments. Time is precious to me now. Things are looking swell now and maybe it won't be long. We will have our homes there and little ladies like you can make some ex-service man realize his effort has been well worthwhile. It is for the kids that I want it over. Fellows like Ken and many of the lads on here. The boys you should give your attention to. Ken mentioned you in *J.E. Campbell* his last letter. He thinks you are swell so I guess all my folks do. It looks like they are all just determined to like you. We all think alike anyway, so I couldn't help but sing along with the others and sort of fall for you too.

I have been having plenty of fun. Saw Tommy Tucker and his band last night. He is plenty good. I have seen several ball games and was out to an amusement park to the high rides Saturday night. Just like a kid going to his first party. Really had fun and I wish you could have been there. Went out to a few night clubs and saw some swell floor shows. It takes all my money but it is fun and I love it. You would to and this has been the best time of my life for the past few months. I have made many friends. Some of them will always be my best friends. One of them will probably be the girl I will marry.

I guess you go to the park often now. It is a swell place to go and I had a lot of fun there. I wish you would have gone down there more with me than you did. I appreciated the time you were with me and I liked every minute of it. I suppose school will be starting soon now. I don't doubt that you will have fun this year. Probably have a lot of things to do. Would appreciate a few letters in your spare time and until you do find time enough to write I will sign off and just wait.

Sister said the pictures were swell. She is going to get one for you so maybe you will be satisfied.

I do want you to write so for this time just goodbye and a lot of luck.

Always,

John

J.E. Campbell MM 1/C

August 24, 1944

Hello Delphia,

I got your most welcome letter, and say it took you a long time to write. You always have things to write about + I don't. I am glad you went to camp for young people must have some sort of entertainment in their lives. I guess you were glad your girlfriend moved back home and you two should have a lot of boyfriends with the car and all. I haven't forgotten my school days. I was a student at that old school once or did you know?

I am afraid my leaves are over for some time. I have been very lucky in the past few months and spent some of the best days of my life. I wouldn't attempt to say when I will get home again but the way things are going now two years is a long time. I wouldn't want to wait two years but I have before so it won't be anything new. Don't let your age worry you any. It doesn't make any difference as far as I'm concerned. I only want you to understand that I don't expect you to figure me in your love life. Things are sure to happen to you. School romances and all that stuff. If you hold back because of a guy in the service you stand a very good chance at missing out on a lot of life. You don't kid guys like me. There isn't any use of trying. We can't be hurt like we once were and I guess we don't expect anyone to sit around and wait. Should I come home and find you still thinking I am a swell guy, then will be the time for me to make my play. So don't think I didn't care. Wasn't trying to kid you along or anything. I wasn't and I won't. You couldn't lie to me and get away with it. I have been around too much. Let's just say I know you thought I was swell + it goes double for me. You can write letters and help me along *J.E. Campbell MM1/C* out here. I will write when I can find something to say. We will wait and see how things work out so don't be so final in your letters. I never give up not even when the odds are against me. You don't know me to well. I have a very bad temper. I drink, go out with all type of girls and I have been pretty wild. I want you to know that and I think you did. You can't compare me with those kid brothers of mine. I don't stack up to their standard. They were my idea. I guess that is why I am so honest with you. It is the only way I can be knowing how things were. That is why I wouldn't hurt you in any way. Why I will be sure of everything before I make a move with you. I want you to try and understand and if I go the way he did I won't feel too bad. He was the best guy I ever knew. A patriot who never knew when to give up. It hurt when I was out with you to realize that you were his idea and to find you attracted to me much more than I should allow. Maybe you can understand better now Delphia. I don't figure you as a baby, but as the sweetest girl I know. We got a long way to go yet, and it won't be easy. Just keep your fingers crossed and hope my luck hasn't run out and maybe I will be home again soon.

I just got your last letter + had to stop to read it. It hurts to know that another guy has gone along and I know how his mother must feel. I knew him but not too well. He was just a kid when I joined the service. You seem to be trying to make me jealous about your boyfriends. Just don't tell me about them and then I won't feel so bad. They are a lucky bunch of guys and I am just the property of Uncle Sam.

Say you must be trying to get me to say I care a lot for you. I do, Delphia, but please understand that I can't get serious about anyone now. When you care for a *J.E. Campbell MM1/C* guy that means better. It also means you just don't go out with anyone. You don't want that + I want you to live a little. Find out what goes on in life and then maybe we can agree on things. If you expect me to think you care you will have to write a lot of letters and you don't have to keep them friendly if you don't want to. I am not a rock of granite. I am just a sailor trying to tell you I am not your type.

I would like to have you with me when I hit some good port. Show you the highlights and really have fun. Show you why I always want to come back. My idea of life and why foreign ports just don't appeal to me. I have seen a lot of them you know. We would have a swell time. You would love it and so would I.

Well, it's getting late now. You won't be getting many letters from here and so please write to me even though my letters don't get there so often. Maybe that is a lot to ask but I will appreciate them an awful lot. I won't be going to nightclubs; ball games and all those things so don't worry that some girl is taking my time. It will be you who can have fun.

You will get the picture. That I promise you, and I guess I can trust my sister. She promised to have one made for you. By the time you write again school will have started so here is wishing you luck. Would like to be home now but seeing as I am not, they can't keep a guy from dreaming. So now until the next time just happy dreams little girl and you are breaking my heart for sure.

Always,

John

J.E. Campbell MM1/C

Sept 10, 1944

Hello Delphia

I got your last letter and was very, very glad to hear from you. I am afraid you are just a little jealous and please don't be thinking I write to any of those girls back home. I went out with them and I didn't tell you that I didn't. I believe I told you. I don't care about them and never did. You wouldn't understand why I go out with them. I also told you Anna Mae and I were through. I write to other girls. Girls I have met since I came into the Navy. Very good friends but that is about all. I doubt if I was ever in love with any girl and these years in the service have aged me plenty. I live a fast life for I can't expect much in return. You don't understand the ways of people as I do. I know how they can lie, and be cheap and just no good. How they can hurt and make a person not trust anyone. You are young and know little about life. You had a crush on me and there aren't many guys left back there. It won't last and I don't expect it to. You are very pretty, very nice, and very real. Maybe I kidded you about being a baby but I knew better. I didn't want to be around you too long. Things would happen and maybe someone would get hurt. You just aren't for me, Delphia, so I don't get my hopes all built up. Nice girls don't interest me much. A plain statement but that is it all written down for you. Maybe now you understand why I don't want you to be anything but my very best friend. I wouldn't go out with you all the time if I were back there. You couldn't pull away the things I have learned in the Navy no matter how you try. Pick a much younger guy one who hasn't been in long and you will be on the high *J.E. Campbell MM1/C* road to a happy home.

Delphia, I am sorry about the letters. I also don't like to think he was unhappy. No girl could cause me to be and yet I expect you hurt the kid plenty. I understand honey, but I doubt if Ken does. Your letters to me had been very sweet. Herb couldn't put his feelings on paper and people back there told him things. You don't understand how it affects the kids out here. If you did you wouldn't think about letting them down. I have seen them cry and just sit about for days when their girlfriend got married. Those things have caused me to get hard and bitter towards the people in the States. I don't intend to lecture you for you know your feelings. Girls cause these boys to be sailors like me. The guys who live while they can. Sometimes I wonder why I ever dared to risk going out with you. Didn't you know my rep? isn't so good there at home.

I guess you will be glad for school to get started. Sure, hope you have fun this year. Nothing like the old school days. I haven't gotten a letter or card from Pug and I am plenty mad. It wouldn't hurt them to write. Bill + I were pretty good pals when we were kids together. I guess we can't forget those days. I have always liked Pug. They can make me feel much better by being around when I am home. Even the baby liked me and they have him ruined.

Well, I have a watch in a few minutes. Settling down to Western stories, radio programs, and regular sea routine these days. Life is dull but your letters brighten it up some so please write to me more often. Going to sign off for this time baby. So, bye now and don't forget to think of me when some other guy is kissing your lips.

Love,

John

P.S. I know stamps are a problem so I am sending you some.

J.E.C.

J.E. Campbell MM1/C

John Campbell in Uniform

Del Wininger at the age of 16

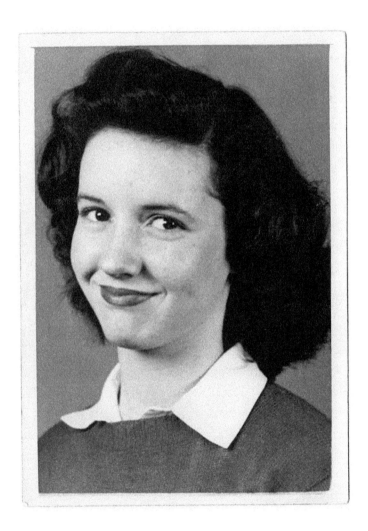

Sept. 26, 1944

Dearest Delphia,

I expect it is about time that I write to you. All of your letters come at one time and I had written, but maybe you hadn't gotten it yet. You are the only person who has ever written letters to me so often, and I couldn't overlook that fact even if I wanted to. I like to get your letters Delphia, and I think you are one swell girl. You can chum up many of these dull days that are ahead of me out here, and I am going to appreciate that. There is no telling how long it will be before I get home again. I don't expect it to be soon and I don't guess I care too much. I don't expect you to understand why because I know you do not understand my attitude on life. You haven't known me long and you draw a nice picture and say that is the guy. Well, honey, you had better get wise before I stop trying to tell you that things wouldn't work out. You know I might decide that I like you very much and then you would have me hanging around when this is over. I think you are playing a game. Trying to see just how far you can go and get away with it. Girls do sometimes and with so many guys that you know I don't understand why you don't go for one of them. I wouldn't mind being around. Don't get me wrong. It was nice to be with you. You were something I couldn't explain, but I will tell you once more that I was at my best. I was sober home and happy. Maybe you don't understand what I am trying to get over. It is just that I am no good for you, Delphia. It is better that you know that now for I would tell you when I get home anyway. You understand that I have reasons to always be very nice to you. You are making it tough for me to explain my feelings. You couldn't be like other girls in my life. I wouldn't permit you to be. You are so young. I can't understand how you expect me to take your letters and actions. Ken wrote and I guess you stand plenty high with him. He is an ok guy, Delphia. Some girl will be lucky when he gets home.

I would be foolish to tell you these things if I wanted to play around with you, but I want you to know me well. We can be friends then and no one will get hurt. I have been around a lot *J.E. Campbell MM1/C* since I joined the Navy. I know the score on life. I have seen several foreign ports. Drank, played cards and has been just no good in general. I have went out with any number of women, most of them bad. The type you don't know much about. Been around with some I liked very well to. There is a wave who thinks she still has the inside track on my future, now I have to explain all of this to you. I won't reform. Even you couldn't swing me and you should know that. Please, Del, just for once try and grasp the idea I am trying to put over. I have told you more than I ever told anyone about my life. From now on it is up to you. Anything you want to know I will tell you. I will write when I can and I hope you keep the letters coming this way just as you have. Sorry if I have disappointed you, but I still say there is more of me getting hurt. Maybe I would come back and fall in love with you. It could happen very easy for a lot of guys will get their downfall before you stop breaking hearts. It would be tough to get stood up. I guard against that. It happened once but never again. Maybe I have built up a self-assured life. Could be I never want to come home for good. I am a regular navy man you know. Not in for the duration like most of the guys back home. Suppose I wrote and told you I had four more years in the service. You would feel different then wouldn't you? Better think it over, sweetheart. Let's don't let a school girls romance be your downfall. There is a few things about navy life that gets every sailor. No girl can be sure of these guys. I don't know why I tell you all this. Here I have the sweetest girl I have ever known telling me that she loves me and then I write letters like this. Gosh, I don't know why I don't hand you a nice line and take advantage of the first impression I made on you. I will take back that statement, Del. I do know why and so do you. I don't never want to forget and I won't. Anything I ever tell you will be honest and the truth.

Say, I guess you are well settled in school now. No doubt it is a lot of fun and let's don't worry that pretty head of yours about what girls I had dates with and wanted to take places when I was home. They never had a chance. Frankie isn't bad. She is a lot of fun so don't be jealous of her. I only kidded you about her. I knew her before I came home last year and some of the others

J.E. Campbell MM1/C back there to. I never took any of them serious and I guess they don't think much of me.

Too bad the boys can't come out with a winning football team. They very seldom have much in football. Basketball was always their best. We didn't win a football game the last year I played there and the team was a good one. Then they were plenty hot on basketball. I think we lost about four of the thirty games played. I saw them win the tournament last year when I was home. Those kids were good and I think the '41 team must have been better. The boys out here that played there like to hear that the old team still wins. Lindy has always been crazy about ball games. He is a swell guy, Del. My favorite brother and best pal. He has had a tough time along the line. Not too many people know him well. I guess I do and he can tell you more about me in five minutes than anyone else will ever know. I owe him a lot of money now and I had better get it paid. He liked Anna Mae very well. So plenty mad at me because of her. She won him over, and no other girl I ever went out with did.

I am glad you like the pictures. It will have to do you for I don't have any snap-shots and won't be getting any soon. Do you think lipstick is the proper thing to put on letters going out to a sailor out of boot camp? Gosh, Del, that is the first time any girl ever pulled that one on me. You are impossible at times. Are you trying to get me to feel serious about life, maybe just having fun, eh? Well anyway this is much more than I ever write and I have a bad finger to. I hurt it today and it is plenty sore tonight. I guess it will be stiff tomorrow and it hurts. So, for this time just "goodbye" and best of luck always.

As ever,

John

J.E. Campbell MM1/C

Del with Dog

Oct. 10, 1944

Hello Delphia,

Seems a long time since I wrote to you, but there just isn't much to write about. I got a letter from you today and the only one for two weeks. I guess you are plenty busy with school in full swing. It was always a lot of fun for me and I wasn't a bad student. Would you believe that I pulled B+ for four years and was number ten in the graduating class? Not bad for a guy who played basketball + football as we didn't have any study period. Lindy said the team was good this year. I guess you go to all the games. We like to know that the boys are still going to the old school. Coach told me when I was home in '42 that more men had enlisted for military service from that school than in any other part of the state. Something to be proud of. They were a fine group of young men.

Del, I don't mean to be hard to understand. I only want you to understand why I like you. Why I appreciate your letters and why I say you should go for someone else. This war is a long way from over. I don't expect to get home again soon. It may last three or four years. Can't you realize where I stand. You can make me fall for you and then let me down. I don't want that and I guard against it. You don't know me to well. I wasn't around long. You are pretty. A swell sport and I liked you a lot. I didn't fool myself about you. It was swell having you around. I liked the way you did things, your eyes, your hair. You can be a knock-out so why waste your time on a guy like me. Most guys would fall in love with you very easily. I did, but I just knew you weren't for me. Maybe I will change my mind. The time element will be that judge. I read a lot, honey. Lives of people and books doctors wrote about people. I know the score on life and you have a lot to learn about. I have told you things and still you think I am ok. From now on

I tell you nothing. If I come back and you still feel the same as you do now then you win. You won't hurt me if you don't. Just tell me *J.E. Campbell MM1/C* the truth always for facts is how I deal. If there is some other guy then you take him. If not then stick around until I get home. I will get married when the war is over Del. I want a home to live in, a wife to have and other things that go with people who are happy. I am willing to try hard but suppose I don't click. I am old on this job. I probably wouldn't be way easygoing. I might go off the beam and pull something crazy. How do you know we would make out. Maybe you wouldn't be so fond of me if I were out of the navy and around a lot. Those things will have to be talked over, honey. Don't be too fast to judge me. I might disappoint you.

I don't suppose there is much doing there now. I haven't written to Bill as yet. He just never writes if I don't write first. Bill is a swell guy and still is. He and Pug were nice to me. I would like to be with them more.

Listen honey I will be writing to collect those kisses. I still remember the ones on my last leave. Those eyes haven't left me out here. You always seem to be searching me for something you couldn't find. Did you expect to break through these years of my life and read them. Find the type of person I am. Maybe you did, but I doubt it. You know I will never try handing you a line. You are too honest and trust too much. With me that is ok. I wouldn't hurt you in any way but some guys will be trying to kid you along. Trying to make you fall for them. Have fun and go their way. Do you get what I mean Del? Anyway, that is about enough of that. Think I will see the movie tonight. We have one aboard and there isn't much else to do. I saw "Kings Row" last night. Was one swell picture. Just about all I can muster up this time, honey. Bye now and be a good girl and write to me often. You are the number one booster of my morale. Best of luck and don't forget me.

Always,

John

J.E. Campbell MM1/C

Oct. 22, 1944

Hello Delphia,

Just about time I pester you with some more of my chatter. Been sometime since I have gotten a letter from you, but they will catch up in the near future. I hope you are not getting disgusted with me for I only try to tell you things that are best for you to know now. Del, it isn't that I don't like you. You know I do, but there is some very big problems in my past life that wouldn't permit me to allow you to become involved with my personal life just yet. You are the type of girl that a guy would fall for. The girl most guys would want to marry. It is just that I don't figure anyone along with me now. I won't hand you a line and I won't play around. You know I will be honest and give you the truth. Maybe I like you better than any girl I know. I am certain you were nice to have around. Most girls would find me some different than you did. I suppose that is why you think I am a swell guy. Well, the next time it would be different and you might not like me so well then.

I guess you are having your troubles there in school now. Anyone as cute as you are shouldn't have trouble getting an A if you have men for teachers. Wouldn't mind teaching you a few things myself. I bet you would be a willing student or would you, Del? Do you go to the games? Lindy said the team was big and should get better as the year goes along. Don't get your heart set for anyone of those star football players. I wouldn't like that and would be just a trifle jealous. I do want to know you much better. Would like to spend some more days like the last one when we were together. That was swell and I liked every minute of it. You were something nice and lovely and it took me back to days when I was out of the navy. I remember you out here, honey, *J.E. Campbell MM1/C*, and don't ever think that I shall forget. You can be some guy's past war dream and he will have one of the sweetest dreams going.

Things are rather dull for me. I get a few books to read and a movie sometimes. Not much to do aboard a destroyer but put in time. Sometimes a week seems like a month. The mail is the only great help. It cheers a guy up to get letters from a girl like you. Those letters are swell. Through them I can figure out your moods. I am very good on judge of people, Del so don't try to kid me along to much. You write far above your age. I am surprised at you but I think you are nice. Go ahead and have your fun for I like it. Just don't get caught at your game.

I guess our old stand-bys at school are just like always. They are two really swell persons and I never missed the pleasure of a long talk with them when I get home. I guess they consider the boys in the service much as they did when we were in school. I doubt if they really see the thoughts that lurk through our minds. Know the changes that a long period of service has caused. They are two I won't forget and a few happy memories still remain.

Look, honey, I might be busy out here for a while and don't feel hurt if you don't get letters often. You do know I must be good and no girls to clutter up my life. I like these letters you write very much. Please don't stop writing them and I will try and make it up to you when I get home. I just don't have anything much to say and a lot of people to write to. I am sure you understand. Now I am going to sign off for this time so "bye" and lots of luck.

Always,

John

J.E. Campbell MM1/C

Nov. 1, 1944

Hello Delphia,

Just a few lines so you will know I haven't forgotten. You don't have to worry for I won't let you down. It just takes your letters a long time to get out here, honey. Maybe you haven't been writing much, but only one letter in about a month and that isn't much when a guy begins to miss someone and the thing he dreams about. Maybe it sounds silly that grown up men have daydreams, but I expect all of us out here do. We all expect to be home again and wonder about the future. Wonder if we can make a go of life after service time. How has this life changed us and I know I have been changed very much. Six years doesn't seem long to some people but it has been a tough grind for me. I am not my old self and I guess the folks have noticed the change. It might be a hard job for me to change again.

Del, don't think I would ever stay from home if I could be there. Sure, I have seen a lot of places and had fun in most of them. When given the time I came home and stayed until I had to leave. You think life there is dull but that time home was the happiest days of my life for me. It was fun just to rest, be with my folks again, and enjoy once more the things I learned to love long ago. Then I liked some of the new friends I learned to know this past year and you were swell to me. Don't never think I don't care for you. I do Del and always will. There will be a bond of friendship as long as we exist. To want more would be foolish for me. You are very young and the sweetest girl I know. I guess you won't mind if I dream of you a little now. What the future holds is too uncertain. Someone far superior to you and I hold our fate. We still have a long way to go before we reach Japan. I will probably be getting along in years then and you will still be young. We cannot recall time. The past is gone and only the *J.E. Campbell MM1/C* future belongs to us. In the days ahead we profit from our mistakes in the past. I have lived much. You so very little. I am wise to the ways of life and of people. A very good judge of those whom I meet. You must still learn much and I only hope you are smart enough not to let someone fool you to much. Del you know I didn't try handing you a line. Didn't tell you I was in love with you and all of that. I can't explain how I feel about you. I am confused and all mixed up about you. Maybe someday we will realize why and then we might not. All I know is you are a dream in any language. Swell to know and something to remind me that we are lucky to be Americans. I guess I know that a lot of fellows have girls like you except they plan to marry them when they get home or they are married now. Me, well honey, I don't dream that far ahead. You might not like the idea and I am to human to have my hopes shattered about me. So, I will remain a sailor. Live my today and let tomorrow bring what it may.

You mention girls in your letter. There has been some in my life just as anyone knows people of the opposite sex. Some I really cared for. One back when I was in school and I guess she sort of put me on guard against falling again. She was my dream girl for a long time. Road many a sea-going smile with me but I forgot. Her letters went overboard and with them went my dream. She wasn't for me just as you are not. We just didn't make out and I haven't been very serious about any other. So, you can rest at ease about others. You got more on the ball than any I know, honey. You can be first up on the list of a lot of guys. No need to worry your pretty head. A lot of fellows will be heart-broken before some guy snaps you into order and takes you out of circulation. I know guys and you are sure to make a hit with many of them. The best of luck Del and I envy the lucky guy.

I don't see why you find school tough. I always liked those days and had a world of fun. These people *J.E. Campbell MM1/C* were and still are my best friends. We shared a few years together and now they are all over the world. So far, my pals have been lucky. They are in this war everywhere. Italy, France, North Africa, China, and out here. Everything from privates to Captains and the army has most of them. My best pal is a Sgt. in Italy. Haven't heard from him for a long time. He is married and his wife has a baby now. Something for him to get back to. Things that maybe I want and can't expect. We are much alike, he and I. Will probably see a lot of each other when we get home again. I expect the deacon will be seeing us at church on Sunday and we will just be an average citizen but deep down we will be proud of our buddies who couldn't get back. It is for them that we go on for now. That Del, is hard facts. That is why I don't care how long I am out here. We have no right to enjoy the pleasures of being home all the time when they gave their all that girls like you and just America in general could go on as being a free people. Free to love and live. Choose their friends and go their way. I guess you don't enjoy flag waving but I just want you to know that this is important to me out here.

Say baby, I don't know who gave you any dope on me before I came home. I wasn't very well known there and not so well liked either. I like the impression I made on you but take it easy for I am not that good. The folks think I am swell. It goes double for they are the nicest folks a guy can have. Other people didn't figure me that way so I just wonder who is putting the bug in your ear.

Say, Del, I had better sign off now for Ken will be blowing steam if I don't drop him a line. Be good honey, and write to me when you can find some spare time. Don't let anyone tell you I won't be thinking of you for I will and I will remember everything you stand for. Bye, now and luck to you always.

As ever,

John

J.E. Campbell MM1/C

Nov. 15, 1944

Hello Delphia,

I know you are furious because I don't write so very often, but honestly it is hard to think of anything to say. Just got your letter with the pictures and they are swell. You sure are a pretty girl, honey, and other people think so the same as I do. There is one guy on here from Alloy and he is pretty anxious to meet you. He is one swell kid and we may get home together someday. I am not trying to show you off on my shipmates but if you would like to write him, I will send you, his address. He is only about 18 and a snappy-looking Kid and those pictures of you have him curious.

Del, I guess you just don't understand my attitude on life and a lot of things. Most of all I would before you are through. I wouldn't dare get ideas about you myself. The crush you have will wear off and you will be all the happier then. I know I am silly for not pressing the advantage I now have for I have never doubted that you like me. Don't think I don't wonder a lot about you. You are swell and I have always liked you from the very start. I won't forget out here and I will always wish I could share back time for a few years. Honey, life is a game of chance. In some ways, my luck has always been good. With girls mostly bad. You hint about other girls but there is only one more and you that has a chance of stringing along with me. I wouldn't tell you there is no one. She is a wave and I do like her very much. She isn't the girl you are though so you shouldn't worry to much. I never dreamed that I was playing with *J.E. Campbell MM1/C* romance by writing to you. Never figured you would give me a second look and now I refuse to allow myself to become involved in the love affair of a girl so young. I warn you Del, I am not so easy to handle as you may think. I am very set in my ways and you don't know me so well. Let's don't argue for we must always be the best of friends.

Say now we will have no more talk about failing subjects and getting out of school. Anyone who will try can get by and I don't believe you get bad marks. And all subjects to be afraid of history is the last one. Why anyone can make good marks in that. Even I, as thick headed as I were, passed history. But you do have a lot of fun going to the games. Who is the lucky guy that holds your hand on those long rides back? See I know all about those things and maybe I am a little jealous. Lots of fun for you though, isn't it?

Say, Del don't always be wanting me to destroy your letters. I just never do and won't. They are sweet and nice every one of them and I wouldn't mind anyone reading them. Honey, I will never forget that Kid and you know it. Maybe that is why I never want you to really fall in love with me. People would talk and maybe I shouldn't have the one thing he wanted most. Del those are hard things to say but out here it won't be easy. Your letters cheer me up and I really look forward to them now. I promise I will write and you can bet I would like to see you again. Just let's don't mess up a really great friendship or cross bridges before we reach them. The future will work out some way for us so now until the next time I will say goodbye and luck always.

As ever,

John

J.E. Campbell MM1/C

Nov. 27, 1944

Hello Del,

Just a few lines to you tonight. Been getting a lot of mail and more from you than anyone else. Thanks a million, honey, and I think you are swell. I am afraid my letters won't get back too often for we get a lot of sea duty now. Maybe you won't mind and keep writing for we get mail more often than mail going out.

I know winter is on back home now. I am afraid I like winter very much and if you could realize how much time I have been in the tropics you would know why. Sure, spring and autumn is much better but me I will take them all. I miss the things that go with seasons. There is so much fun there on the farm. I didn't appreciate it much when I was there but gosh, how I have missed the old place since I have been away.

Those pictures were swell. I must tell you that again and it brought comments from the guys. Maybe you will get to know one of these kids when we get home. He hounds me plenty for information about you. It will probably be some time yet and then they always transfer men. I like this crew very much though and get along better than ever before. I could do worse so I might be on here a long time.

The last mail brought bad news out here to me. One of my old school pals was killed in action Booty Mays. He was captain in the army and pilot of a heavy bomber. I doubt if you knew him. One swell guy but aren't they all? One more home wrecked by this damn war. I knew all those kids who were in that car wreck at home. I guess it wasn't so pretty and they say some of them will never regain their health. Those wild parties always bring trouble and they were always the one to try them.

So Gwendaline is married and out of the running. Bet *J.E. Campbell MM1/C* I know one guy who won't like that. Chuck Parker had a crush on her and how. Then you know I was deeply in love with her myself. Anyway, I had a few dates with her and she was nice. Guess they will all be married women when I get home and I will be doomed to the life of a bachelor. It isn't fair to us sea going boys and there should be a law because they will have to pass a bill in Congress to get enough girls out after the war to form a cheering section when we come home. It is only proper that we have one day of hail and how are you? When we get finished and come home for good. Let the liquor flow free and the band plays for it is going to be the one happy day of my life. Del, I won't forget the guys who aren't there. They will be there with us in the spirit of victory. Alongside me for the rest of my life will be the memory of the greatest guy I know. That is why you couldn't be anything but tops on my list. Someone will come along for you some day but if they don't, I will be around to see you get a square deal. Anything that you want to know or anything that I can help with. You can be the party to welcome me home. Would you like that? I don't have any other girl and you wouldn't let me down would you? Getting foolish now but got to have something to write about.

You shouldn't let any ideas Bill might have interest in you. He can only see one way and won't change. We used to fight plenty because we both are stubborn and I didn't always win. They don't write to me but I will write them soon. It doesn't matter Del. You know my folks and there has never been a serious argument among us. There is a deep devoting, fun loving, feeling between us all. We have our own pets. Every one of us and they were all proud of me when I came home on my first leave. It has worn off some now with all the men in the service but I still rate with them and for them, I mean to do a good job. Bill had a way with the girls before Pug grabbed him off but she really slammed him up. I know a lot of girls who *J.E. Campbell MM1/C* had ideas on him. Would wish at times that I could make hits with them but I didn't get by so well. We used to go around together some and I don't forget. He is a swell fellow and I would like to be with him more. They say the kid is just like him. Trouble for someone and how. Pug has always been nice to me. I like her best of my sister in laws. She never said one word about anything I did while home on leave. She let us drink and have fun. They like you too and I am glad for I know you don't have many people there to go around with.

You wanted to know what I remember about that leave. All of it, honey. Every moment of the best time of my life. Don't think I forgot you. Never that. Remember how shy you were and the first time I kissed you. Gosh! But that was funny. I believe you were scared of me. Anyway, it is getting late. I have to leave with more nonsense than ever so I will sign off for now. Bye baby and have fun. Be thinking of you so don't forget to write.

Always,

John

J.E. Campbell MM1/C

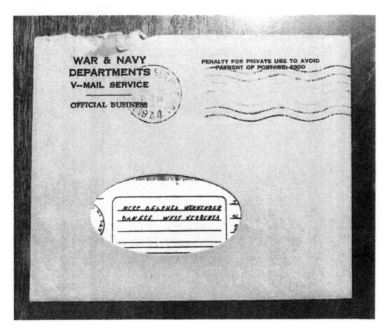

Dec. 7, 1944

Hello Del,

How is winter and my girl now? Notice the date and it has been three years since Pearl Harbor. Thinking back to the day when I huddled about the deck of another destroyer and heard that awful news it doesn't seem three years. Then to think of all the things that have happened it seems much longer. No Del, I won't try to tell you how long I think it will last. My opinion is no better than yours and I may have given up hope. It won't be soon and of that you can be sure. I will be gone for a long while and I thought that you wanted that. Giving you a chance to grow up, baby. I will be home and find you going out with some guy or even married. When are you going to stop kidding me? I can't believe you are serious even if I want to. You do write more than any girl ever did and I know you don't get many letters. It takes them a long time to get back. If you keep that up maybe I will have to believe you for no girl will continue to spend much time on letters unless she really likes a guy. I just can't figure out why you like me. I didn't go out with you much. Maybe it is because you are so young and haven't been out with many guys. I don't think you know the score. You think you understand me and you don't. You don't understand any guy. Most of them go out with a girl for a good time. If you think different then you are foolish. You have something on the ball honey, and a lot of guys will fall your way. Suppose I told you I never want to get married. I guess that is what you want. Maybe then you would drop me or would *J.E. Campbell MM1/C* you?

You never look at life very serious. Do you know I will be out here six months after the national emergency is over. The war could be over for a long time before I get out. Then I will have to find a job and get set out there. That would take a little time. I will have a few dollars mustering out pay and that is all. Maybe I can make a go of it and maybe not. If I don't then something else will happen. While I am there I will be trying to live some of the life I have missed. You could wait but I won't. It will just be that way so don't be getting ideas. I wouldn't be satisfied to sit around and play hands with you for a year or so. Me, some girl who isn't so nice would be with me so you see it won't work out. You wouldn't want things the way I do. I know what you want and I say we just couldn't get along. You wouldn't give in and I wouldn't be around. It is better that you know, Del. I don't want you to expect something and have it go wrong for you.

I think Ken will go home soon. He will be giving the girls some of his time. Better watch that he doesn't cause you to be swinging his way. He is one swell guy and has a line of gab. About other girls I know. I don't write to any at home. They just don't interest me. Haven't written to Anna Mae since I saw her last. We are finished and I told you that. Some other girls do write once in time months so. I don't see any cause for you to worry your pretty head. You are the only one that wants me around so I don't have much to say except I think you are crazy.

I guess you do have fun at school. Did you get to kiss all the boys "good bye" when they went to the army? I *J.E. Campbell MM1/C* guess I missed all the fun by not getting a war time send off. Maybe you can save a few kisses for me to give this guy a war time welcome home. Think you can, honey. That won't be all I want but it might have to do. You are one nice armful and I know that. Someone taught you things and did a good job. I expect you get plenty of practice now. Lots of fun playing about as long as play is all. I went to high school once although some wouldn't believe it. I remember all the good times we had. Lot of loving and all that. Don't tell me you don't slip out on the crowd to spoon with some guy. Everyone must do that to have any good times. It is life and most of all the fun of living. No one is serious and everyone find those times to their liking. Just watch your step baby and save your loving for me.

I expect you get tired of this line of gab. Got to fill paper with some kind of talk so please don't be angry. I wouldn't have you change your letters for anything. I like it even if I don't believe all the things you say. Miss you when you don't write so maybe I am just a little in love with you. Anyway just as much in love with you as any girl I ever knew. I would like to see you now. Talk with you and laugh and just feel that someone cares.

Del, I don't know just when you will get another letter. Things are never certain out here but please don't slack up on the writing. I will be getting your letters for they come through. Bye now and best of everything to you.

Love,

John

J.E. Campbell MM1/C

Dec. 12, 1944

Hello Del,

Guess it will be a few days now before I get any letters from you but I will write anyways. You would keep me very busy if I were to answer every letter you write. I guess it is a happy surprise to find someone who writes when I don't answer. The folks don't always wait for letters now and I find letters much more often than ever before. I appreciate that for though I have been away from home for a long while it still lingers close to me no matter where I go.

I know it is snowing and cold there now. We get the news every morning and today it said the Mid-west had a lot of snow and I can bet you have plenty also. I miss those winters and I never cared about how cold it was. The boys in Europe must have a hard time fighting in all this cold weather. Their winter offense will pay off and it might be over in the spring. The B-29 promised big things out here. I don't kid myself any Del, but we are on the last lap to Japan. It might be much longer than we think for they are stubborn fighters but then most everyone thinks we can give them the works now. I guess we are tired and want to get home. I know most everyone is anxious to try the civilian way again. Not many of us hasn't ever heard the names of these islands that have been taken since we started an offense. They will go down in history now with the blood of American boys to write the headlines. The blunder of a government and may they not be so easy going when victory comes this time.

I guess you are planning for the holidays even now as I *J.E. Campbell MM1/C* write this. Going to be number two out of the states for me. Number two straight in the third since the war. It won't be much fun, but folks at home can be sure that we wish them all the happiness Christmas can bring. I guess the folks will have a tree up for they always did. Then the dinner mother had was tops with us all. Those were happy days and it's been a long time. They can never be the same again. Maybe I wish they could but that is gone now. Another mile-stone passed in my life. Something to look back to. Something now to know it is worth the tough going so others can enjoy those things.

Mother sent me a cake but it hasn't gotten out here yet. I was sure it would be in the last mail but had to settle with a letter from you. It wasn't a bad trade and yet would have been more fun to have both. Greedy, don't you think? Well, it is your fault if I want a letter from you every time mail comes aboard. You are stealing my heart baby, and it isn't too much of a job to keep me guessing when I am miles away. I want to get home and hear you say a few of those things you write in your letters. I will know then if you really mean them. Most girls wouldn't go to so much trouble for guys like me. We really aren't worth it you know. Life has been rough for us and we learned the hard way. There will always be a hard, cold hand to govern our actions. Honey, I don't trust, and I don't think, don't act and just not the guy, fellows you know are. No matter what you read and hear the fellows with a few years out here are different. They are going to be hard to handle so you have a warning. If you choose one don't say you didn't know.

I know some of the guys you went around with. They think they are hot stuff where girls are concerned. I guess maybe you *J.E. Campbell MM1/C* fell for them or anyway liked some of them. I think you told me you did. Well, you understand I wouldn't care. I have lived too long to worry about what has happened in someone's life before I knew them. You can have a world of fun now and I know that. Foolish if you let it go by. Don't think I don't give a hoot what you are doing. Listen, honey, I would like to be there every minute of your time. I want to know, you better. I will know what you do now from the people at home. You step over the line just once and I will hear about it. They always know about parked cars and late nights. Trips girls shouldn't

44

take so you better give out with straight talk or go off the line. I don't expect you to stay perfect but I do expect the truth always.

Remember that last day I was home? I keep thinking how your eyes looked and wonder what you were thinking. I can't forget how you cuddled up close and you were so nice to have around. That day you almost won me over, honey. I was afraid of you. Funny thing for me to say but it is true. You were all that I wanted then and I don't think you knew it. Just stay that way until I get back and I promise to be around more. I won't tell you I will stay. You might not want me to. It is like that song "Time Waits for no one". Well, I doubt if you will either. Anyway, here is signing off for today and luck to you always.

Love,

John

J.E. Campbell MM1/C

Dec. 23, 1944

Hello Del,

Guess I had better be getting a letter off your way. The last one from you was all of one page and I don't like that. Make them anything you want but no notes. They don't go over so good when a guy is a few thousand miles away. I know you haven't been getting letters way often. They just don't get off the ship. I thought even you knew the war is still on out here now, but from the hell, I caught in the last mail almost everyone has forgotten. Your note was dated Nov. 29. I got it yesterday and was damn glad so maybe you and I sail the same mailboat.

It is almost Xmas now, honey. Going to be a dull one for me just as the past few have been. Nothing to send you, home or anyone. It is no good when you can't be where all the happy memories of the past still remain. I could send the folks money but I have an allotment going home. Starting another one to pay Sis and save a few dollars for my next trip home. I expect to save a few hundred dollars so I can really have fun. Go down Charleston way and really have full benefit of my old home state. Would you like to go along, Del? I guess not for I am afraid you couldn't see my way of life.

Mother sent me a fruitcake but haven't gotten it yet. I think we will get mail tomorrow and maybe the cake for Xmas. I never get but just one slice of my favorite with a mob of hungry guys about and I enjoy the same privilege when things come their way. The guys on here are a swell bunch of fellows. I don't know just how long I will be on here but it is my best ship so far. I can't say I don't have time to write for I do but those letters you write leave me in a hole. Time is no trouble but something to write about is. You never say much. A lot I can't comment on anyway. Del, I will be going out with some *J.E. Campbell

MM1/C* girl study when I get home. You could be the one but I don't think we would get along to well. People at my age live some different from younger folks. Things you don't think right is only part of our life. You would have to go my way, baby for I wouldn't go yours. Better think it over now and have your mind made up before I get home. No wedding ring for my girl yet. That you have got to understand and maybe Del you have better call it quits before we go any farther and one of us gets hurt.

I guess Ken will get home soon. Some kid and I suppose he will see you. Better watch out for that lad. He has a line of gab and you are one pretty girl. He likes them that way and you could cause him heart trouble or I am no judge. I guess I want you around when I get home and I am a little jealous of the guys who date you now. I like you honey, and don't forget that. There isn't many I have cared much for but you are my best girlfriend now. You are the one I write to most and the one I want to get home to. Time could change things but I don't think so. We will have a million things to talk about and a million more to do when this is over out here.

Well, it is getting very late now. I am very tired and the ship is rolling very much tonight. For this time I will sign off and please don't forget that your letters get to us even though we don't get mail often. Be good baby and may the new year bring you a happy 1945.

Always,

John

J.E. Campbell MM1/C

Jan. 3, 1945

Hello Del,

This day starts a new year and this note to you will be my first letter of '45. Bet you like to know that for it means I do think of you often and I appreciate all those nice letters you have been writing. You will never know how many letters I have started to you and then torn them up before the finish. You are getting so personal I find it tough to think of things to say. A million things about you I remember each day and find myself wondering why you stay around so long. I was sure your crush would wear off in a few months. I could see playing along with you and I liked it. Now you are getting serious and it is a sure sign someone is in for a let-down. Honey, this war is so far from over. If we could set a date for the day I would get home then it would be different. We could plan and be sure of things. There just isn't anything for me to stand-by. It might be months but will probably be years. Don't you understand why I don't want you to get yourself set on me. The idea is foolish. You are just a babe-in-arms. The sweetest girl I know, and I am not going to spoil you any. No, I am not afraid to fall in love with you. I guess maybe I have been for a long time now, but I know enough to control my emotions. Life is a span of years and not a few days. We live in trust out here. Trust that we will be able to establish ourselves in civilian life and grasp a few things that we dream about now. Your letters are a treasure to me. No girl attempted to write so often before. I know you don't get mail so often. I do the best I can and if you find that not enough then it will be beyond my control.

You seem to be having a swell time. Someone picked a swell looking cheer-leader. Guess I am missing out on something now. Would like to be there for I remember all the fun my old class had when we were finishing there.

Now you talk about a run in with Frankie. She doesn't have *J.E. Campbell MM1/C* anything to compare with you so I don't guess you are having much trouble getting her out of the way. I thought you were the only love Curtis had and now I find he has strayed. Guess I will have to straighten him out. What is the trouble with people still in school? They can never seem to make up their mind just whom they really like. Why I thought that I was top on your list and then you write about boyfriends. I am a bit jealous with all these miles between us I will say he has the advantage.

You shouldn't worry about the wave. I know. Blonde but that doesn't matter. She doesn't care too much about me. Just good friends. I guess you have all the girls topped with me anyway. I told you I like you a lot and isn't that enough. Maybe I should get myself a book on how to write love letters and you would like that better.

I don't know who gave you the idea that I might get married anytime in the near future. Don't have any affair that serious unless I could talk you into thinking I am a swell guy. Maybe that wouldn't be a bad idea but you wouldn't listen, would you? Can't blame a guy for dreaming and you would be one nice real dream. I look at your picture and wonder how you are changing now. Can't help but remember the quick-silver behind those eyes and the way you smile. Anyone ever tell you that you cuddle up nice and you are nice to love? I didn't think but I wish now that I had. You can tease Del, and no girl will make me forget. Guess you were what I wanted and I am thinking a lot about getting back. Getting some more teasing if that is ok by you.

This gets worse as I go along. You got me going your way now and I hope you are happy. Just let me know when you have enough and I will drop off the line with no regrets. Have to sign off now and go on watch. All I get done these days. Sure, will be glad to see the old farm

49

again. Any place that I can stay for about a month without anyone to disturb me. Bye now and best of luck.

Always,

John

J.E. Campbell MM1/C

Jan. 10, 1945

Hello Del,

How are you, honey and what's doing back home now.? It seems like ages since we got mail and I am getting behind on the dope. Your letters will be there when we get those sugar reports aboard and Del, if you ever fail me now, I guess I would just about stop trying to think the job we are doing is worth while. I have been afraid all along the line to believe I could be anything to you. Now I want to believe things you say are true. I am sure our problems can be worked out when I get home again. I guess the navy has given me enough experience in engineering that I can hold my own on several jobs. I don't want to go to sea again. If you are sure of yourself then I am all ready to give life a try. Maybe you will be the answer to what I need. You may find me hard to understand but we will get by. You had me hooked the first time I came home but I wouldn't let you know. I didn't expect that you would ever so much as consider me. I am glad to be wrong and Del, I miss you a terrible lot now. Keep wondering what it would be like to have you out again. Make plans and really be friends. I guess we wouldn't be friends either. It goes farther than friends when a guy began to take a girl like you serious.

I made out an allotment for sixty dollars last week. Every month that I stay out here it builds up and when I do get a leave, I will have some money to spend. I have enough to pay Sister what I owe her now so what I save from now on is mine. Del, I can't get anything for you out here. It isn't right to pass up Xmas and all but what else can I do? I could have sent you money *J.E. Campbell MM1/C* and then maybe your dad wouldn't like that. I don't know him very well so I just let things ride. Anything you want I will see what I can do. I have my first time to stay along with any girl and I find it nice to let you be the one.

Therefore, we must get to know things about our lives. I will tell you things I want and you can tell me what you want.

When I get home, I want a car and a gun. You go along with that, honey. You will always be first. There will be some small town to live in and I guess some of my old pals to chum about with. I like sports and movies. Read magazines and books and play cards. I like to hunt and fish and I always enjoy driving about through the hills. The old farm had a place in my life that will never be removed. My mother is something very dear to me and my dad the most respected man in my life. My brothers and sisters have always been swell. Lindy and Macy are really grand. Herb respected above anything in my life and Ken is a grand kid. Nothing has ever come between any of us and nothing shall. One more very bad weakness at home. I don't think you know Gloria June. Well, she is all of about ten years old now. Blonde and blue eyes and the sweetest kid I know. She is my pick of the family and I can't forget things she did. It was Gloria that always wants to see me when I get home. My campaign bars she just had to have. She doesn't know where I have been but those ribbons mean a lot to her. Sometimes I wonder what I can say to her in a letter. She seems so much a child and yet she does expect me to write. So, you see my uniform has more than one admirer. This stuff doesn't make sense I guess but I get this way at times.

They seem to be stepping up the war out here. New reports bring in new invasion dope and more about those famous *J.E. Campbell MM1/C* B-29 bombers. The Japs seem to have lost their power in places and it is great news to the vets out here. These fellows are tired of war but they go on because they know there is no let up until victory is won. When the peace is signed then I have earned the right to come home. The right to seek a haven of not from War and the World. The right to have you and if you agree to take you as my companion in life. If you don't then that is America. I go my way and find someone else. These fellows fight that you might choose your way of life. The people of the States owe so much to so few.

Look baby I am getting way tired. I have said a lot in this letter that I didn't dare say before. From here out it is up to you. Someday I will be home. If you think waiting is worthwhile, I would be glad to know you are staying around. There is a lot you will have to know about me but I won't write it in letters. I won't build my hopes up to high but Del I do love you. That should matter some to you and I won't give up easy. You are just a babe-in-arms and I don't expect you to understand me to well. I will take my chances now. And I do hope I may win your heart my way. Thanks a lot for all the sweet letters you write and let me say that if you plan on handing me a line you do one swell job. Bye now and write more often. Those letters are my best bet to get home.

Always,

John

J.E. Campbell MM1/C

Jan. 27, 1945

Dearest Del,

Just another effort to write this letter to you. It must be at least the sixth attempt for you have me tangled up some and now I don't really know what to say. Maybe I was trying hard in those letters to get something over. I did not at any time doubt but what you are very innocent of any bad thoughts and you didn't have to remind me that you are what I would consider a nice girl. All along now I have been trying to make you understand that our code of life has a great difference. I have lived a life these past six years that has had no one to straighten me out. I cannot recall those days and they have influenced my life. You do not belong to that side of the road and it would be hard for me to picture myself as up to your standard. This war has affected my attitude on life and I doubt if my thoughts are as stable as they once were. I really don't know what I expect in life now and I am certain that any plans will just have to wait until the war is over.

Del, I never wanted to tell you of the days we put in out here. It doesn't matter much. I just get older but you would have to know about places I hit before we met. Maybe if I tell you in plain language just what I mean you can understand why I wrote the letter that caused you to sort of give me hell. When I came in the navy, I was just an average guy. High School graduate and expected the navy to take me places. It did and I haven't been sorry. In California I began running with a gang of guys. Swell bunch of fellows. None of us were very serious about any girl and we got along. We drank some and *J.E. Campbell MM1/C* and had a lot of fun out there. Then we came east to the Atlantic side and a trouble zone. It was 1940 then and San Juan was our base. There is where we started out to the bad. We drank to excess. Didn't write home much and it was a tough crowd. Most of us ended up with court marshals and regret them to this day. Some of the boys snapped out of it then. They came home. Got married and became sailors instead of bums. Well, I didn't and my pal didn't. We hit Brazil and South Africa. Saw the ways people live. We saw the worse for that was what we looked for. Then came the war and it hasn't helped matters any. Right at the present nothing matters too much to me. I might be home sick but I doubt it. I just don't seem to care much. Most of the old gang is split up. I see them sometimes on other ships, a lot of them won't be back. I think I have lived far past my years and you can't catch up.

I may as well tell you this to. There were women in every port we hit. Not your type for sure. We went out with them and figured it all in a good time. They are my kind of people. You are not. You couldn't be so foolish to think I will change. You saw me at home and at my best. I liked you and respected you because of a personal matter. Let's let it stay that way. You would be foolish to take a chance with me.

Del, I know what you would want. A home some place with friends and a car and places to go. Maybe a baby sometime and a guy whom you can trust to the limit. You are just as you said a nice girl. Well, you know why I won't try and cover up to you. I could and you would believe me. No, I tell you straight and how you decide must be your affairs. The war may last two years yet. Then it would take me at least one year to get me straightened out with a job and all. The affair looks *J.E. Campbell MM1/C* rather dark to me. You are very young and can wait. I don't get younger out here. Should I be able to call back one year of my life those big brown eyes of yours would have gotten a very cold stare every time you looked my way. How was I to know you would be TNT to me? A school girl taking me over after I have hit the hot spots of half the world. It has been nice knowing you, Honey, but you cause me an awful lot of trouble. You are ruining my plans so why don't you just drop me a line and tell me you have been fooling me all along the time. You stay the way you are and let me find other girls to go out with. If you don't Del, it might cause us both a lot of trouble.

I never told any girl this. Never had to before but even if I love you, and I think I do, it is only fair for you to know. There are so many guys there and it would be so easy for you to slip out of my life now.

Del, I can't expect you to understand why I write all this. You are very special to me. You can weigh all this and then make your decision. I will say now that it is in all fairness to us both that you sort of give me an answer to all things that you can't bypass it and neither can I. Your letters have been very sweet and I hate to bother you with this stuff. It is better that I tell you now than later and anytime you want to be my steady girlfriend then you are in. The idea that I don't want to come home to you is absurd. Every day you get more important and it is only our opinions on life that we must straighten out.

Going to sign off now, baby, so going to have a good time and write real soon.

Always,

John

J.E. Campbell MM1/C

Feb. 1, 1945

Hello Delphia,

What doing at home + how is my baby now? You are taking a lot of my time these days. Three very sweet letters from you in two days now, and one just can't ignore that. I don't like them so short, honey. Some of them don't say much more than notes I once wrote to girls in school. Maybe there isn't much to write about but I have a very limited subject plus a censor looking my letters over and I always find something to write about. Sure, you write more often than I do. You don't have as many people to write to either. Sweetheart, can't you understand that letters is all I have between me and all the people I know. There aren't many girls. Not any that you know, except maybe Eileen Kesler. I write to her sometimes. You don't have much to worry about when I get home. Guess I will have to wait for you to grow up or do you think you are a woman now? I guess you don't like some of my ideas. Del, Honey, don't brand them wrong as yet. With you + I things will go different. To me you are an idea and I never told you I wouldn't get married. I only tried to get over to you that it will take time for me to get myself settled when I get out of here. That I wouldn't be going out with girls of your type. Must have been slightly off that time so please am I forgiven.

You know I don't care about you going on dates. What else is there for you to do? You sure don't have to account to me for anything. You have been sweet Del, and if you should change your mind anytime now then I still have been helped a lot by just knowing you. I don't want to take up your time. These are the days you can never forget and if you don't have fun, it is your fault. Dates are education to you. Guys are mostly all alike except some have been around more. I *J.E. Campbell MM1/C* guess I know the score pretty well and it is possible some of my remarks were rather rude. You wouldn't try kidding me, Del. It won't work and I know you like going out with guys. Let's don't argue about it and I sure, don't worry about you. Didn't you like me telling you I liked you to cuddle up in my arms? You had me softened up plenty and it would be easy to love you, baby. Would you mind if I say you have something on the ball? Those other guys have the advantage on me now but I will make up for lost time when I get home. You owe me a million kisses now. A million sweet words and a lot of loving I expect to collect. Are you going to mind, Del? No guy could resist you for long.

I think Bill gives you a bad impression of me. I was not such an imp as he pictured. Rather shy with the girls and he knew them all. I drank some and helped him in his fights. Even went out with him on dates. Pug had her hands full with him. He had a way with women and I know several, whom thought he was a swell guy. He worked and furnished me with money and I went to school. We got along well and still do. Just wrote him a letter a few days ago. He is soft hearted as they come. Very easy hurt and not hardened to life as I am. He will trust easy and I don't. I learned the hard way + Bill has never had to learn. It is a happy family there, maybe the things I dream about and never expect to have. Guess any guy would be proud of a kid like the boy they have. Pug is swell. I never knew a person I like better.

Say, Del how about some more pictures sometime? Have to see how you are growing. And about shortening your name. No one told me. Did that on my own because I like it that way. Sorry I wasn't the first guy to think up the idea, but maybe I can be the first with you on other things. Guess Ken slings you a mean line. Look out for the kid. He is TNT. Going to sign off now, honey. So, bye now. Be good and don't forget I expect those letters now.

Always,

John

J.E. Campbell MM1/C

Feb. 6, 1945

Dearest Delphia,

Well here goes again. Still getting a lot of letters from you and the last mail a Valentine. Very cute and I like the verse inside. Wonder just how much of that you meant when you sent it out here to me? Everyone, and you included seems to have a gripe at me for not writing letters. Honey, you get more letters than I ever wrote to anyone else. I guess I have been away from home so long that letters doesn't matter as much as they do to the younger guys and fellows who are married. You are very sweet to try and keep me cheered up out here. Don't you know it's going to be a big letdown to me when this little affair blows up in my face. Be honest, Del. You don't expect it to last and I don't but it has been lots of fun. You are much to pretty and nice for me to be interested in. You would only cause me trouble. Heart trouble, honey and I don't want any more of that. Some day when I come home then you will know why I write like this. Maybe you can understand why I will always like you so very much and why I couldn't let myself be fooled into thinking you could be in love with me. You've got notions now that will wear off. I guess there were things about me you like. Sister, claims I stand in good with several girls if only I would focus my attention on them. I guess she likes you Del, but she is wise enough to know that her sailor brother has been around too long to get tied down to home on any short notice. I like my folks but she is a very swell Sister to have around when a guy feels low. She can write letters to pep a guy up and does. She will never know just how much her letters has helped the guys so close to her since this war has started. I don't say she doesn't approve of my interest in you but she does think you are a little young for me. I am apt to listen to her advice for after all she know about marriage and things I don't know *J.E. Campbell MM 1/C* about. You see I am a little afraid of being a civilian again. A guy forgets a lot in six years. A man in the service don't do his thinking much. The service does it for him. Guess there isn't much use saying these things to you. I just get myself more fouled up every letter I write.

Sending some more money home tonight. Be all squared away on my debts and starting on enough for a leave when I get back to the states again. Things look good now and it might not be so long until this is over. Maybe I will have enough to get me started on a job out there. Sure, hope so for I want to make good once I am cleared from the navy.

You seem to be peeved at me sometimes. Guess I am harmless and I do my best to keep our friendship going. I might step over the line and make some crude remarks at times but I wouldn't doubt you Del. I don't trust anyone much, but I am no judge for you. Someone else claimed you there and as I write this tonight there is no doubt in my mind that I am holding my end of this deal out here as he would. Don't you understand honey, that he lives along with me yet? I must not let anything keep me from being the guy, he figured me for. It isn't right to you to keep bringing that up. I couldn't possibly explain to you how I felt toward him. Maybe that is why I can't let myself believe that I love you. The big question is would it be fair or right. Should you and I judge that or is it too big for us to solve. Del I don't know. I just don't feel that I should have the one thing he would have wanted most. Baby, can't you understand that.

Look this letter has caught me in a depressed mood. Suppose I secure for now and wait until I get some more letters from you. Maybe we can get things straightened out and I do hope so. Bye for now and best of luck to you.

Always,

John

J.E. Campbell MM1/C

Feb. 15, 1945

Hello Del,

Been a long time now since I have gotten a letter from you, honey. I guess they are on the way somewhere and these letters to you are getting to be routine. I just remember that I was home this time last year. Those were happy days and I am looking forward to the day I get back again. The news looks great these days. I don't remember seeing the morale of any crew as high as this one. They know we are in the final lap and with a little luck we will be home again.

Del, you get in my thoughts more every day. I find myself wondering how much you are going to change and what I will say to you when I get home. Are we going to be just good friends or is there something between us that might mean happy dreams to me? You see I worry some about you. You are a problem to me that I can't figure out very well. I don't know what you want or even expect. I have to base my life on sound reasoning now and you are so young that day dreams take much of your time.

When the guys come home again there will be much confusion and many will make mistakes. Only divorce courts and unhappy marriages will result in many cases because the two people involved are not suited for each other. Life will not be so simple. Some of us guys are going to find it tough getting a job or at least one that will satisfy us. Many like myself, don't have girlfriends that have known them long. They are going to make a play for some girl and fast. Most of us write to girls. Yet we can't be sure, about these girls. Maybe they really love someone overseas and we are just fitted in while on leave. Del, I even expect you to be in love with someone. Can't you see I don't want to build up hopes. It wouldn't be fair to either of us. You don't know me well enough and I don't know you. Honey I can't explain in letters what

I expect. It would get you all tangled up and you are much to young to understand my *J.E. Campbell MM1/C* attitude on life. I want a home and a wife just like other guys but I also want to be sure of some things first. You see I don't stay to the idea that my wife couldn't smoke or drink. I know you don't like those things. You just don't live the life I do. I think I should have straightened you out on some things when I was home but honest Del, I never expect to mean anything to you and it seemed absurd that you would ever enter into the place of my life. Now that you have, I am all tangled up and I can't find any way to express my opinions in letters.

If I was to come home now after being out here you wouldn't understand me. I would be different than the last time. You see I dream about liberty back in the states and it sure wouldn't be any church going party. I like to drink, Del. I get around some and nice girls never interested me much. They never lasted long. I knew better than to make a play for you. I wanted to enough because any guy would, but I knew you pretty well. I learned a few things though I haven't been state side much. That is what you will be up against. It is plain language, honey, but what else can I tell you? You have got to figure things out for yourself and you can't have forever to make up your mind. I am not giving you a line. Just telling you I will be the same sea going sailor when I come home on leave. I won't change and if you have ideas that I will then you may as well fold up your ideas and stay home now. I am telling you this now to save myself the trouble when I get back. Honey, maybe I love you but that word doesn't mean the same to me as it does some high school guy. I hold to the idea that people don't have to wait to live and if you don't like my idea then now is the time to say so.

Got to go on watch now, Del. I got an idea about what the answer will be to this but there isn't any use in kidding. We understand each other or we don't. You see my way and I am willing to listen to yours. Give you something to write about. Bye now and be good.

Love,

John

J.E. Campbell MM1/C

March 4, 1945

Dear Delphia,

Just got a letter from you yesterday and was relieved to know you hadn't quit writing. It had been a month and that is a long time to wait for letters that have become important in my life. I don't intend to lecture you, honey. I can't say as I remember anything in my past letters to you to give you the impression that I am growing tired of you or I don't figure you about the sweetest thing in my life. My way of living goes into everything I do or say. I never told you I was anything but a sailor and I even explained to you things I didn't dare have other people know. About the guys, why I was just ribbing you? I am not fool enough to expect you not to go out on dates. All girls do and I am sure you are old enough to know how you will live your life. I wouldn't try telling you anything. I am all mixed up about my feelings for you now. You never mentioned things you want or expect. How can I be sure of anything? I have to guard my every sentence of a letter or you may be offended. If I could just see you Del. Be with you then I am sure things would go differently. This makes the third letter in a week to you. The other two I just tore them up. They didn't sound right and I was afraid you might not like some things I said. For a while I didn't care if you did stop writing. Maybe I even wish you would at times but not anymore. You are the one girl that I want to come home to. The one I would like to try to make happy and I may as well tell you I am afraid I will fail. You can have your pick of many. Some younger then I and fellows who haven't become hardened in the service. With me you would take a desperate chance. I don't want to argue with you now but Del, please don't wait that long to write again.

The navy department has liberated censorship regulation some and I can now tell you some of the things about this place out here.

63

Del you must promise never to mention to anyone there where *J.E. Campbell MM1/C* I tell you I have been or anything about out here. It is important to me that dad and mother doesn't know, at least until I am home again and then it won't matter so much. They would never consider me a hero and I wouldn't want them to. They can't be sure where I am now and if they knew, I think you know how they would worry. This war hasn't been easy for them. Sister writes that another bad shock might be the end for them both and honey, above everything I know they are the two people I love and respect above everything else in my life. To them I must be loyal. Don't think they weren't proud of me when I was home. They knew I had been around without me telling them and though friends would ask me in their presence if I had seen action, they still aren't sure. My dad would smile a little for he knew they didn't get an answer. He liked me for that I guess and mother wouldn't want me to annoy people with my effort to glorify this war. They like you Del and enjoy having you there very much. It would please me if you saw them more often. Just don't tell them things I say and they will never be the wiser.

Well, here is some dope you might be interested in. Most girls like for guys to tell them where they are and it gives me some material to gossip about. You know when we came West. They didn't have us waiting around long. We went to Pearl Harbor and then up to the fleet. Have been in most of the operations in the Philippine area and Formaso. Were in the raid that struck the China Coast. Then we had the misfortune of being in a typhoon and that was one damn rough sea. There is no doubt that things out here are going in our favor and if you read the newspapers, I am sure you must share my opinion that it won't last too much longer. This stuff is something new to me. I saw some doing of this war in the Atlantic even before Pearl Harbor. I don't care to have it last any longer and no one else does. Let me tell you again all I want is to get home all in one piece and I will be a peace-loving man for *J.E. Campbell MM1/C* the rest of my days. The longer I stay out here the more chances of getting home when we get back. Saving over one hundred dollars a month now and for the first time in a long while

I am ahead of all my debts. Sent Sister four hundred dollars to pay her off and from now on my money is my own.

Guess basketball season is over there now. Did you have a good time at the tournament? Bet it is all the talk for I know how those things go as I once attended them myself. A lot of stolen kisses and the girls aren't so shy. Don't kid me, Del? You are much to pretty to miss out on the fun and no doubt you had a jolly good time teasing the guys along. Of course, there is no harm done and you couldn't play with me like that, could you? Those brown eyes of yours can fool most anyone. I wonder how much they have fooled me.

I have just about finished a book by some young woman back in the states. It was her first book and brought her fame along with a good deal of cash. She seems to be the rage there now and the book is a best seller. "Forever Amber" is the title. Was taken from the times of King Charles II. It is hot stuff. Sexy and not a page of boring reading. I guess it would shock you to read it and I doubt if you can find it about school. If I know those teachers you won't. Anyway, I have enjoyed reading it and I must say that England was in a bad moral state at that time.

Darling, I must sign off now and write a letter home. I try to keep these letters as interesting as possible but they must seem boredom to you at times. Please try and remember that I am a long way from you and doing my best to prove I adore you and want you to wait until I come home. Try to remember we don't get the mail out just any day and please let's don't quarrel. Bye now and I will be thinking of you as my times go by out here.

Always,

John

J.E. Campbell MM1/C

March 6, 1945

Hello Sweetheart,

Going to surprise you with another letter. Just got four from you, and Del they were nice. I had to take back a lot of things I had been thinking about you not writing. Those letters were sweet. You came closer to me than ever before. Honey, don't bank too much on me starting to change. I just stay the same except I think of you more often for no girl has ever taken so much interest in me before. I almost believe the things you tell me now. You owe me a million kisses and forever a smile. I just didn't know anyone could be so nice.

I can remember the first time I was with you. Not the time we met but when we were alone. You seemed so young and almost scared. I don't think you were one bit interested at me trying to impress you by my stories of the big cities and foreign ports. You were far more interested in trying to keep me at a distance and yet I expect you wanted me to sort of hold you that certain way. Kiss you just a little and say things I didn't mean then. Remember how angry you were when I would call you, baby. Gee, Del but I wouldn't have believed it then, that you were going to be my first real heart trouble. There have been others for a while but they didn't last long.

You amuse me with some of your questions. Eileen and I have been friends for years. Sure she always mentions Freda in her letters and I don't forget easy. Freda is married now and I am sure I mean nothing to her. It has been six years since I have seen her and I have changed. Maybe I liked her a lot but not as I like you. Del, don't be jealous of girls I know. I have lived to long to let anyone spoil my chance with you. I won't care to see others when I get home. Am sure you can take up all of my time if you care to. Those girls you mentioned there at home. Very few times I dated them. They were nothing I can assure you and it never seemed possible that *J.E. Campbell MM1/C* I could mean anything to them. No, I would rather think that I was just another service man they wanted to play around with and I doubt I made a very good impression.

Del, you always want to know when I can be home again. Gosh, baby what good would it do us anyway. If I were home to stay it would be different. Then we could plan and be sure. With only a few days that wouldn't be possible. I would be trying to live a few days for the time I have been away. Don't you understand I am not seventeen. I am twenty-seven now and have no visions that I am fighting this war for the corner drug store or to be able to see a movie with an American girl. I know what I want when I get back and it might shock you if I wrote it out on paper. Your ideas are not as grown up and your character is higher. If we were married or even engaged it would help but I wouldn't chance that. You wouldn't want it and it wouldn't be fair to you. Therefore, I think it is best I stay away. You can't satisfy me with a kiss and sweet words. Gee Del, don't you see through that. The way I live you think is wrong. To people who really care I think not. Let's just don't talk about that. It causes you to worry about what I think and I am sure you are to innocent to indulge in my affairs. You would only get hurt.

Got a letter from Bill. He is some guy and seems to think you are swell. Don't they all. Sure Spring couldn't be far away for you and I hope you have a merry time. The picture is cute and I like it. Still, I like the others best. Maybe you can send me more this summer. You in a swimming suit and that. Wouldn't mind, would you? Del, it has been a long ways out here and memories are all we have. Is it my thought if I just want you more every day? Honey, I think I love you now and when I am with you again you will get your proof. No one can cause us to draw apart and so now that we agree on all that I am going to say goodbye. Got to get some rack time and I will write again soon.

Love,

John

J.E. Campbell

March 16, 1945

Dearest Delphia,

Just a note to answer your letters. All this letter writing to you is a problem for me. I don't have much to write about and if sometimes they are a little boring, please try and excuse me for I am doing my very best.

Honey, your letters are a treasure now. I find myself scouting them over for some of your pet remarks and it brings a lot of news out here to me. I never knew any girl could be so sweet and I am sure that I wasn't missing any of them too much until you came along. Del, somehow your letters are different. You seem almost real just as if you came along with them at times. Must be this sea duty is getting me down but anyway it isn't going to be a very hard job for you to keep me around when I get home.

You can bet I will find it interesting just proving to you that I do mean you are my girl. I know what I want, sweetheart and you have a lot to learn. Some naughty thoughts you get about me at times I bet, and I deserve them all. Del, don't expect me to be much of a guy. I will give one honest effort but you will have to come through on some things yourself. If things go over then we will decide just what to do. Your ideas are a little too strict for me. I don't kid myself about what you expect. It is a ring and all that goes with it, isn't it Del? You will get it, honey and if the navy lets me get home it will be soon.

I am afraid that just you wanting to see me awfully bad won't get me home this summer. I don't try to guess when I will get back. When we do come stateside it will be a West Coast port and three thousand miles is a long strip of land. There would be plenty of trouble getting much leave so I wouldn't have a lot of time at home. A few days wouldn't be worth the money and trouble because we would just be more mixed up than ever. I couldn't bring you to the coast. Your folks wouldn't allow that and I wouldn't want you to travel alone *J.E. Campbell MM1/C* so don't start getting your hopes to high. It isn't so bad as it sounds. They are transferring men back most every day now. Some of the engineers are sure to go and I stand as good a chance as any. Those boys will get thirty days and probably east coast for most of our fighting ships are built there. Some of the 1/C on here will get rated soon and that will improve my chances of getting off. Del, I like this ship well enough but I just never wanted to see anyone the way that I want to see you. Do you mind if I feel that way about the girl who will be my wife someday?

You know I never figured you would continue to write, and I sure expected your crush to cool off some. I have liked girls before and some of them liked me well enough, not enough to keep trying though, and honest you are hard to brush off. Honey, I wasn't going to forget how nice it was to hold you and how you looked and those things. I just didn't plan on letting you know that you could make me care. It seems to be a game with girls these days and I wasn't going to be a victory for you. If you want to call it quits now you have won, but I think you are honest in all these letters and I do believe you love me just a little. I am sure I love you plenty and if this Uncle Sam of ours will just give me the time, then I am willing to prove to you that this is no line.

The war news looks good but there are still many months ahead of us and how I hate to think of time now. Del, would you want to get married now or do you plan to wait until after the war? I know this is very personal but don't you think I should know. Maybe you are too young to consider that matter. I am sure I wouldn't know just how you feel. All I can think about is that I am going to want you bad when I get home. Hope you have some answers by then and are sure of yourself. We can't make mistakes and honest I love you something terrible.

Been reading a lot of short articles in magazines recently, mostly written by reporters on the war front and they give a very good picture of just what goes on up front and behind the lines. One interested me very much and if folks at home would read that maybe they *J.E. Campbell MM1/C* would understand how the guys out here feel and why they don't write to often. He declared that for every letter a man in combat zone writes that he should get ten letters in return. Even made an effort to explain how they miss their wives and girlfriends and how they have vision of their own loves in someone else's arms. Del, you just don't know what desire and passion means yet. It isn't easy to be pinned aboard ship for months without seeing anyone but the same guys. Fighting men of a combat ship that have grown indifferent to almost life itself. A few years of this and a guy could believe most anything. With you it is different. You can go out with guys and have fun. Desire doesn't bother you much and I know that. Well, I shouldn't be talking about these things. It doesn't concern you and it isn't a nice picture to paint. You know too little of life to understand me and I am afraid that will be the big difference for us when I get home.

I don't know who has been telling you things about me. My birthday and those things. Some of the folks I guess for they are the only ones who knows. Mae is right. I will be twenty-seven and feel about sixty now if it is possible to feel that old. Guess I wouldn't be much use to you after the war anyway. Better get you some high school kid that can keep pace or you will be sorry. Catch you trying that, baby and I might try breaking someone's neck.

Del, I think I have been about three days getting this letter written. Just a few lines at a time and right now, I am way tired. What wouldn't I give for a big white bed to stretch out in and just sleep. This rack of mine lets me nap over some there on four inches in six years has beaten it rather thin. Anyway it will comfort me for a while so I am going to sign off now and remember, sweetheart that I miss you more than I can possibly explain in letters.

Always,

John

J.E. Campbell MM1/C

March 22, 1945

Hello Del,

No letters for a long time now but I will try writing anyway. I know you write honey but the mail just hasn't come in for a while and how I hate this waiting for letters. They mean more than ever before and honest I think I am in love with a dream. That is just about all you are now except letters that always say the right thing. You are so young honey and those letters seem to tell me things. I don't dare consider you as just a possible crazy kid anymore or I guess that I have known better all along. It wouldn't be too bad except I don't expect to give you up so I guess you have a problem on your hands. Trying to find my way clear of this navy, you and a lot of personal problems have caused me to much slip so, I just gave up trying and started telling you in some sort of a way that you are the one for me. I know I will have a tough time getting you from some of the other guys. I guess I will be very jealous and probably not very considerate. I am afraid I will be trying to take up all of your time. You are going to get the rush act sweetheart, because I don't intend to play the field once I am back state side.

I have been trying to get sub school for a long time now and maybe if I wanted to sign up for four more years I could get it. Don't suppose you would consider a man in the service, would you? I guess not and anyway I don't think I care to stay. Can't you see how you have me mixed up and to think that I figured those brown eyes were amusing. Gosh, I never knew I would ever care so much for anyone as I do you.

It was fun being out with you. You were swell and easy to get along with. Just too nice for words and baby you had me going. I would wonder what you would do if I tried kissing you. How you might curl

71

up in my arms and I wondered if you would allow your arm to steal around me to. Del you didn't realize that you were most everything I liked in one. A lot of girls I knew *J.E. Campbell MM1/C* are swell but there were always things about them I didn't like. I couldn't help but love you and you will never know the memories I took with me. How they kindle and live out here and how your letters keep them going along. I don't dare write some things I think about. Just that you take more of my time than I was ever willing to give before and I wonder if you like that?

Say, I heard things about that girlfriend of yours. The guys used to think her plenty nice but I doubt if she is in the running with you. They talk you know and never you mind what sort of dope I get. We all have our fun Del and live our lives. I would like to know her + no doubt I shall someday. Maybe when I come home, we can all get together for a few days of fun. Have to warn you sweet. Blonde hair and blue eyes were my very first impression of something nice not too long ago. If she is all you say she is would you be afraid to have her around with me about. Some people say I am not one to be trusted. What do you think.

Not been doing much recently except getting some long days and these destroyers are rough on men. I think I will be broken and through when I get home. A cripple and then what will you think of the sailor you have a crush on? Guess there will be some life left but don't you ever think of the years between our ages? Don't you sometimes wonder when you realize how much more I have lived? Del, you never commented on things I told you. Don't you believe them or is it that you think I am okay anyway. Most of all I want you to be happy and I wonder if you would be with me. When love dies out some and just the passion that is left in married life is all there is then how will you feel? Maybe that isn't a fair question but don't you learn about people. Know the rotten things that go on around you. Del, I can't write these things to you. I am not going to try but honey I don't want you to get hurt.

Well, here is about the bottom of the page. Going to sign off for tonight. Be sure and write often for these letters bring you across the miles and I love you honey. No fooling!

Always,

John

J.E. Campbell MM1/C

March 29, 1945

Hello sweetheart,

This letter is going to be snappy and to the point for I don't have but a few minutes to make the mail deadline. One letter from you the past two weeks and it was just a short one. Guess you should be over the mumps now. Only babies ever get things like that and you trying to tell me you have grown up. I guess you will be grown more before I get home though and maybe it will be a heart ache that you will be there.

Say honey what is all this talk about the army coming through? Really, I didn't know you were playing other service men too. Maybe I am just your stand-by in case you fail other places. Well, I am plenty jealous of guys that have any luck with you. I don't like to think about you with some other fellow and I damn sure don't want you handing me a line. Del, I give up easy and you had better walk the straight and narrow if you want me to come home to you. I guess you know I am going to hear about everything you are involved in. No one wants to cage you up. I want you to learn and have fun but honest you don't realize how you can hurt these young guys out here. Let these servicemen alone or mean it. Take your choice and if I am on the outgoing line, it won't be the first "Dear Johnny" letter that has come my way. If you are serious about the guy that makes all the difference but if you are not then he is going to get hurt. I guess you wouldn't know how one of these fellows feel when he goes through hell, and has his mind set on something then comes home and finds it hasn't been the same with the girl. I guess maybe you think I have the nerve telling you off like this but it is high time that you make up your mind. You can't play around forever and anyway I am not the playing kind. I know what I am after and I won't be around much if I don't get it. Maybe some other guy would be better for you anyway. *J.E. Campbell MM1/C*

I had a letter from home and more bad news. This last guy was a friend that I liked well. It seems there is no end to the misery this war has dealt out and sometimes I wonder if it is worthwhile. Radio report just came in on the coal miners' strike order. I wonder if those guys know how that effects moral out here. I am a long way from home tonight but were I there someone would be told just how much we are against those strikes. I doubt if it holds up supplies very much but I am under the impression that a cause that our boys give their life for is worth a few days' work and not so much griping from the civilians. It seems to me they would have more respect for their sons and brothers in the armed forces. I guess they just don't care to much how we fare as long as they get what they want.

Don't seem to do anything but gripe at the world in general in this letter. I don't have much else to write about. We were with the fleet that hit Tokyo last month. Things are going our way everywhere now and maybe my luck will hold out a while longer. The boys in Germany seem to be heading for final victory. Gosh, I hope it won't be long for I am getting way tired of being out here. I think about home and you too much now. Baby, you just wouldn't understand how much I miss being there now. You make home almost perfect and I guess someone as sweet as you were almost sure to fit in with folks like mine.

I don't guess anyone will be telling me just what to do with my life but they influence me plenty. You seem to be pretty sure of yourself, little lady. I guess I have gone over-board but I won't be fooled too long. I told you before that no one is going to hand me a line for long and get away with it. Ok I think you are sincere but I can't be sure. Life has been a lot of troubled watchers for me and I am not the type to play innocent with. I wouldn't say you are one to have a smart line but you don't do bad. Just be careful that your sucker doesn't turn out to be harder to handle than you bargained for. Just time enough to get this off so bye now and be good if that is possible.

Love,

John

J.E. Campbell MM1/C

April 2, 1945

Hello Del,

Well here I am again. Back to pester you with another letter. You are sweet, honey and your letters seem to be there every time the mail came in. Guess I am letting that fact go to my head and maybe thinking it means more than it really does. No girls ever bothered this much about me before so maybe I am a sucker for your bait.

You worry too much about girls I knew before you came along. The affairs weren't very serious. Sure, I knew Anna Mae was coming down from New York last year. Del she is one of the nice girls I know so don't start getting bad impressions. It is over now and you should know that. We had to many different views on life. Things didn't work out and that is that. About others there haven't been any that meant anything. Just dates to go around with and have fun. You probably go out with many more fellows than I have with girls. There is a lot of sea duty under my feet these past six years and baby I haven't been having that wonderful time that you have painted up. I have got by and been damn lucky. I had fun in some places but most of that time has been long and lonesome days aboard a ship and there isn't much fun to have here. Darling, these feet of mine haven't touched the good old earth for seven months now and so just in case, you wonder what girl I am handing a line to and what port I am in then you can cease your worry. Only the pin-up girls we get out here. They are a poor excuse but they bring memories and I guess we day-dream better with them around.

I guess I wasn't very well known there at home. I had been gone for a long time and people weren't much interested in me until I came home from the Pacific. I remember you probably four years ago when I was home on leave or I think I do. Anyway, I remember you very well when I was home in '42. Guess no one noticed me too much for I was hitting the bottle very heavy that trip. Then last year *J.E. Campbell MM1/C* it was impossible to pass you up. Pretty girls haven't entered my life so often and Del, you are my dreams all in one. You needed worry about others I know. They don't travel in your class. I am afraid someone will come along while I am away and steal my dream girl for that is about all you are after being gone this long. Maybe I think up some of the things about you. Maybe you didn't show me the attention I let myself think you did and then maybe those letters you write are not all I want to think they are. Yes sweetheart, I am afraid of you. Afraid that you can ruin my life with your playing. You don't understand the way men think after being out here for a while. I don't think I understand anyone or anything.

I can bet spring is there now. Apple trees are in blossom and soon the laurel will be out. Guess you find it dull with all the young fellows gone. Honey, maybe they will be back soon now. Back to enjoy the home they have fought to protect. There are going to be a lot of guys to give you a whirl and I am not to sure, of myself. You could be all wrong about how you feel and I am so sure. Then maybe I don't have the right to have you. Del, there are so many things that you don't know about. If this falls through then me life will be in one bad mess. I would have been satisfied in the navy but for you. Now my enlistment is up and I am riding for duration. When I get out it won't be easy to find a job and get going. I guess I will have to have someone to help me along and if I can't grab you off fast then I might not make out so good.

Look baby, these letters are getting terrible. There just isn't anything much to write about. If I write often then you know I do care. So then maybe you won't mind all this mixed-up mess. My brain just doesn't click at times. Going to sign off now so bye sweetheart and be good.

Love,

John

J.E. Campbell MM1/C

April 11, 1945

Hello Honey,

Been a little time between letters but the mail came through today and letters from you and home. Getting closer to me all the time Del and, honey and how I do want to get home. Home to the peace and quiet of the old farm and the little girl I love. Going to be a lot of hours to spend their next time I get a leave. A million things I want to do and a lot of loving you owe me. I expect to find you waiting there and I think we understand what we will be up against. Maybe I do know the angles but you were a good student and from all indications I wasn't your first instructor. You were good at teasing a guy and I like more than teasing. I guess you know just what you want, Del but guys like me don't stick around long. This war has left me pretty much on the go. I want a girl that goes all the way and you might as well think that over before I get home. These letters are very private between you and I. there is no reason why we shouldn't discuss our personal feelings in them. Sex is always a big problem and very much so in war time. No one waits for marriage these days and you know that. You and I will be facing the same problem for darling, I won't be home to stay next time. All we can hope and plan for is a few days. I love you Del and that is honest from down deep so you need not worry about me giving you a line. If we talk about the feelings between ourselves then both of us will have a better understanding of the affair before I get home. I told you girls are nothing new to me and I guess you knew that anyway. To stay in the same bed with one shouldn't be anything new to me. I think I am going to far with this stuff. Going to want your answer on these matters and just in case your girlfriend is looking over your shoulder she is getting some very personal dope. If you don't like this kind of stuff now is the time to say so. If I can cut my letters down to just friends again and my feelings along with them. This stuff I am going to let you decide while I am out here. You won't be influenced by my personal contact now and Del don't make any mistake. Let it be final one way or the other. That way I won't be living under any false pretense and I will know just what to expect when I get home. Other guys and their girlfriends have understandings so why shouldn't we? At least I would have something to write about. Maybe I surprise you but I bet *J.E. Campbell MM1/C* you expected this. Del, can't you understand? Hell, I guess no one that doesn't come out here will ever see through guys like me. You don't have to hug your pillow at night and wish it could be the one person you love. It is easy for you to go out and mingle with people. Even a date now or then and you don't have to think like I do. Other things keep you jumping all the time. There isn't any use of me trying to kid myself or you either. I wonder if some other guy makes out with you. I think about a million things and the life I have seen hasn't helped me to trust anyone. I never wrote letters like this to any girl. I don't know how you will take this but if we are to plan for any future I do think we must be sure what each expects. I am being very frank with you. At least you will have the chance to drop off now and that is all on that subject until you give me an answer or your viewpoints of these doings.

Ken wrote that he was getting a leave. I doubt if he and Dreama will have much of a romance just yet. Ken plans on school after this is over. He is a talented youngster and I am sure doesn't plan on letting girls getting to much mixed up in his life. He does well in the navy, but I don't think he likes it. No one does for all hands are damn sick of this war. I expect you have seen him by this time. I believe he expects to get shipped out when he gets back.

So, you read "French Man's Creek." I understand it was a good book. Been trying to get it myself. The picture was one of the tops of '44. Haven't seen a good movie for a long time now. Too much underway time. I tell you a good book, honey. Read "King's Row" or get "The Strange Woman." They are both top sellers. Both of them are very good. Sexy in places but you can get a lot of dope on living from that type of books. "Forever Amber" was a little too far along even for war time America. It was far to forward in places and many cities have banned it to their book sellers. The sensors will have to do a lot of cutting before a picture is made. I enjoyed every page of it though.

From the reports I get from home strange things happen there now. They write that a deer has invaded the farm and it really makes me think my home is in a wilderness. Wouldn't be surprised if someone *J.E. Campbell MM1/C* doesn't make short work of that one. Hope it stays there until I get home and maybe I can knock it off myself.

Expect you will have much fun during the last few weeks of school. Guess you will find some guys that will interest you plenty and a little petting party will be in order. To well I remember how the stories leaked out when I was in school. The old school romances were all the go and a lot of them ended up in marriage. I wasn't a very well-liked guy so the navy caught my interest. Romance didn't seem to go with my type. I wanted some travel and I got it. I wised up to the ways of living and Del you can't change me. Either you go my way or we call off the whole affair.

Been rather busy out here. We were with the carrier task group that carried operations at Iwo Jima and I made a bombardment run on Okina Daito Jima last month. Guess you follow the news. Anyway, things looked good out here and in Europe to so maybe victory isn't too far ahead. Look those places up in the map and you can see just where your sailor is.

Del, I think I have written enough for this time. Getting sleepy anyway and mid-night is going to roll around to soon. Going to say so long for this night, sweet. Hope you aren't offended of this letter. These things I want to know and see no reason why you can't tell me now. So, bye now honey and have a good time.

Love always,

John

P.S. Do you want to be my sweater girl?

It ain't the sweater

Don't think for a minute

But it is the things

That you have in it.

J.E. Campbell MM1/C

April 20, 1945

Hi Del,

Well here goes again. Getting to be a habit this letter writing to you. Guess it is only fair because you do write very often and I would miss those letters a lot should they stop now. You are very sweet honey, but I expect I will always call you baby. It is my favorite name for you and then that is about all you are. Some day you are going to wise up and find out just what a no-good guy I am and then I won't have anyone to string this line to.

Things have really been gloomy the past week. No one likes to think that our own president's death will affect this war any but there is doubt about Mr. Truman. Gosh, I hate to think about staying out here much longer. Damn this navy and the war. What wouldn't I give to be home and with you now. I never thought of any girl much before but I do you Del. I want you more than I have ever wanted anything in my life. It is rather hopeless, I guess. I know you aren't going to see things my way. I am not going to blame you any. You are too young and trusting for me to spoil. We can't quarrel in these letters and straighten anything out so let's don't try. I have given you too much straight dope now. Honey, if you don't give up now I don't think you ever will.

Streaming miles are going up but still I have no hopes of being home soon. Big thing goes on out here now and they need a lot of navy. I am not griping about doing my part for some guys have given much more. There are times I don't like to think of the guys in the states who will never get out of there. Got my opinion of them but then there are always some types of people who don't have what it takes.

Been reading an editorial by senator Taft from Ohio. He is really raising hell about these eighteen-year-old boys going into a combat zone. It does look unfair to them and it is. There is little that can be done about it. Replacements must be sent up and those kids are the ones that are left now. To bad they have to go so young. Doubt if some of them ever had much life. A lot of them don't last a week. Those are the guys that were your schoolmates last year. *J.E. Campbell MM/C* The guys that girls like you kid along in letters or tease a little while they are on their last leave. You didn't realize how scared the kid was or how close to this hell. War seems a long way from our home but it is only a few days when they really move. That kid that was almost afraid to kiss you is now up against the dirty killers of Japan or Germany and he is still not tough enough to kill. Therefore, lots of them won't come back so don't make it harder on any of them by handing out a line. Give the line to me and have your laugh. I can take it and they can't.

Maybe I am off on this stuff but I don't know. I don't blame them for drinking and living fast. Don't blame them for trying to make any girl they can. They have a right to American women if they caught theirs. America they are fighting for but in America they are refused a drink. In America they want them to go to the U.S.O. a few weeks out of the front lines and death. Yet we expect them to be soldiers and many of them are the best. No if they must fight as men they should be treated as such. They have won their spurs so let them wear them. To them we owe more than to our other men. They gave before they knew the worth of living.

Guess old W.Va. is blooming under spring weather now. Would be good to soak some of that sunshine and mountain air into my bones. Be nice to hold you in my arms and let you tell me all those things you dream up. Let you tease me a little and say things you will never mean. You can drive a man crazy Sweet but I like it.

News report just came in and they say the Russians are only ten miles out of Berlin. Let's hope it won't be long and those kids deserve much credit. News is off and music of all songs here is the one they are playing "Give Me A Girl in My Arms Tonight." Del, it is give me you in my arms tonight and honey would you like that? Going to sign off now for it is getting very late and I need some shut eye. Thanks a lot, Sweet for all these letters you write and remember I love you baby and here is the best of everything to you.

Always,

John

J.E. Campbell MM1/C

April 24, 1945

Hello Del,

Here goes again with a line of chatter. No letter from you the last mail, and I think that I write more letters than you do now. Should be your answer as to how you rate because I wouldn't spend so much time trying to make that crush stick if I wasn't sure that I want it to. You are a little imp for having me so mixed up, but I love you, honey. If I keep telling you that then maybe you will believe it someday. I never wanted anyone so much and I didn't think it possible for the memories of anyone to stay so long. Maybe it is because you know how to write letters and keep them out this way often. I doubt it though. I think it is because you have what I want and you can bet I will be all out for you to. Your letters don't change a lot. You are still getting around my questions. Guess you don't trust me a lot and yet what harm can come of letters. There is a few thousand miles between us and just a spark keeps you close. A woman can always change her mind. Maybe some things are too far along the line for you. Del, you can't understand the emotions of any man that stays out here for months. There is no getting away from the things they want. If a girl wants to hold a guy she will have to give and baby don't forget that. I don't want you to mix anything I say. It is important that you know my views on life. I will get what I want or drop you off. I don't intend to play around with any girl. I guess I would get married now but you would be taking an awful chance and then I doubt if you want that yet. What do you think? Maybe we should get together on some of this stuff. Honey, you never give me anything to work on there and yet you get angry if I don't write this stuff.

The news gets better every day. Don't see how the Germans can hold out much longer. I guess the top command over there is going to wise up a few of our senators on just how bad the Germans were. They have been terrible and the Japs are worse. We can't say just how much cruelty has been dealt out and some of the dope we get I wouldn't pass along to you. It is a known fact their war prisoners and civilians have been burned alive. They starved the people and forced them to live under terrible conditions. Committed mass murders and nothing stood in their way. Now you *J.E. Campbell MM1/C* wonder why an army fights for a command like that and I can give you some points. The German army did as they pleased in the countries they taken. They drank and ate the best. Young girls were put in places to entertain them and when they weren't in battle they lived. They have no creed of horrors anymore. It is the duty of a German girl to have children to turn over to the state for cannon bait in later wars. They believe in free love and home is nothing to them. No nation can live that way for long but they caused a lot of trouble while they were in power. Our boys still believe in home and the girl they love. If she lets down that trust there, she isn't worth being an American and a lot of those have. We get some raw reports in the magazines out here and I guess you know that we get mad. I could give you some cases but I won't. Honey, if ever you get out of line, I will find it out and it won't be very easy for me to take. I love you Del, and I want you for myself. You are so young that I am afraid of times that I will have to get used to having you around. I am jealous of you and I don't mind saying so. Come a long ways since you entered the picture and you are the cause. If you cross me now, I will have a bad trouble. I just think those things can't happen to anyone so sweet as you.

Bet you had fun with Ken. He is a lad the navy won't change and I know the folks were glad to have him home a few days. Guess he will have a dozen new girlfriends now and most of all that longing for the place he and I love best. There is no place like home. Just to lie on the lawn in the spring sun and eat the home cooking that mother puts out would be a lot. To have a lovely young lady to tease you is to much to think about. You wouldn't pass up the chance to kid Ken a little would you. I hope you didn't because it would be a big game for him to try to crowd in on his sailor brother some. I think I would come out on the winning score so have your fun. You can bet I would want lots of loving from you now.

Del, I can't even hope to know when I will get home. The Taussig will be a year-old next month. She has shown well and has eight months out here. I would say we can expect to be back before another year and of course all hands and putting hopes in getting state side *J.E. Campbell MM1/C* much sooner. No one can tell though and I expect a lot depends on how much damage the Japs do to our fleet out here. Don't count them out of the war yet. They are tough customers and we are in their backyard now. Plenty of ships don't live a year so I guess we have done well. Just hope we can bring this little baby under the Golden Gate Bridge and never mind how long we have to stay out here. This stuff is nothing new to me. I knew what it was all about before. I promise you it won't change me any and maybe when we get home that most of us can stay.

Guess everyone is doing some farming there now. Bill seems too busy to write or maybe he hasn't had time. They all let me down and I wonder how I ever made out without someone like you coming through all the time. I used to go weeks without letters from anyone and now if you don't get one letter in every mail call then I get hard to get along with. Be good to the guys on my watch and see that I get that letter. They have to live eight hours a day with me no matter what mood I am in.

Harold Hanshew is state side again. Four months of advanced schooling in Oklahoma. Sent me a picture of his baby girl. Sure, has grown since I saw her last year. He was going to bring Phyllis out there for two months. Swell guy and I like Phyllis. They showed me a swell time in Norfolk last year. Treated me swell for the bum I am. Maybe someday I will get myself a wife. Interested baby or do you have other plans.

Look I am beginning to write to much in these letters. They will be sending them back for more postage. Got enough money to fly home if I can ever get the leave. If I should get ten days or less don't know if it would be worthwhile. A lot of that would depend on my honey so what you say you be getting me lots of dope. Going to sign off now so bye Sweet and keep all your loving for me.

Always,

John

J.E. Campbell MM1/C

May 1, 1945

Hello Del,

Gosh, three letters from you yesterday and today and they cheer me up, honey. You are doing a very good job of letter writing and I appreciate every single line you write me. No one has been that much interested in my welfare before so if I do like you more for writing it is points for you. Takes letters at least three weeks to get out here to us and I have a time remembering the things you might refer to in your letters. Sometimes I forget a lot of things I say in letters. If the past few have you a little angry please try to reason out some of that stuff. I have to think a lot out here and you are my biggest problem. I have been frank and told you the truth all the time. These last letters were so nice. A little different than others you wrote. Del, I like the things you say. You would be a sure hit with most anyone and you had me overboard long ago.

Expect it was fun to tag along with Ken + Dreama. Ken is a swell guy and the navy don't change his type. I am a sailor, Del. The slap-happy boys that have been in here to long for their own good are my type. We have traveled. Roamed about and had fun. Seen some action through the years of this war and most of us are damn sick of it. Right now, I would take a little house in W.Va. and you. That is the way my dreams run and yet there is a hard road to victory and that all important time element can't be thrown aside. Might be two years or longer yet. Things look swell in Europe but these Japs are tough to deal with. It will be over when the navy figures my job is done. I am a regular. Trained the best possible and still young. The navy can't teach to many fellows like me and we can't expect it. If I haven't lived up to your standard in the past I still earned my chance to string along with you if I stay out here. Those boys in Europe will be home soon. Home for a leave and a lot of them to stay. Hope you don't have any heart-trouble over *J.E. Campbell MM1/C* there for he might shove me out of the picture if he got home first.

Del, I don't know why letters take so long. I write to you almost every time the mail leaves the ship. Sure, we will know where we stand when I get home again and of course we are going to have fun. You owe me lots of loving, sweet, and I am going to collect. Don't let other girls worry you. They don't stand a chance. I know what I want and I guess you are it. Got some money saved up now. Enough that we can go most any place and maybe gas rations won't be so bad and things will be better all the way around. Our fun will be just what we make it. You and I have a lot to plan and a lot of things to decide. It is a long way home but with someone like you being so nice to me then I guess some of those miles sort of go away. Everyone has a right to dream and if my hopes are set on you then I can't go wrong.

You mentioned danger out here. War is a serious business, but I have been a lucky guy. This old tin can have a charmed life the way I see her and some of these days we are going to bring her home. She will have her glory, bars and tales of hardship and it won't be anything new to me. Some of the boys are heading state side for new construction. Lucky break but they rate it. Honest, I don't know when I will be home again. Be there just as soon as they let me though. There is a lot more there now than last time. There is the girl I love and the one baby I want to see more than anyone in this old world. You are my baby honey, and I want you to save your kisses for me.

Del, I have worked hard today. Going to be a movie in a few minutes and they don't come to often. Plenty tired but I won't pass it up. Guess you won't mind to much if I sign off now and I will write again soon. Bye now sweetheart and may you have a pleasant and happy time this summer. Be thinking of you always.

As Ever,

John

J.E. Campbell MM1/C

May 7, 1945

Hello Del,

Two letters from you today so I suppose you rate a line from this end. I think you are getting spoiled by all these letters and you are certainly taking a lot of my spare time. Baby, I never get tired of your letters and I miss you more than you can know. Other girls aren't so important. I write to some of them but they don't travel in your class. Guess I am yours if you want me to be and you get no bargain on the deal. Sometimes I wonder why you stay so long in my thoughts. No one has ever had me so mixed up before. You are a little imp for treating me the way you do. Guess I was putty in your hands and you knew it all along. Having your loving now and when do I get the brush off? Can't believe anything so nice as you could happen to me. Someday all this dream-fest is going to get blasted away and I will find myself out on the limb with you sawing it off.

Del, you know damn well I want to get back just as soon as possible. I got you to come home to now and things have just got to work out. The questions I have asked you aren't hard to answer. It is just that you won't decide as yet. No one blames you for holding off. Everything is yours to give and I think you are afraid that I am not the type to stay. I am honey and I promise you that. At first, I figured you wanted to play along and have fun. Now I know better and I find myself day dreaming and counting the days to when I might get back.

Honest, sweetheart, you in my arms would be dreams come true. Sure, it was nice before. I can't forget it and those days found me just watching for a hint of teasing in your eyes. I couldn't see myself meaning much to you but if your letters give out straight dope it looks as if I landed and solid. I wouldn't dare tell you the things I think about at times. Dreams you ask? Gosh yes sweet and some day they *J.E. Campbell MM1/C* will be real. I will tell you about them when I come home. Some of them might be naughty. Bet you wouldn't oppose of that. Say, Del can't you understand the things I mea?. Maybe I am tired of the Navy. Tired of roaming around and of drinks and girls. Would it be a surprise if I told you that it is something more settle that interest me now. You and I together and the chance to prove that we can be happy is enough for me. Honey, maybe I don't say the right things in these letters but I try to get over my points. If you don't make an effort to straighten me out on some things then these letters are a waste of time. Maybe I have been pretty blunt but I don't want you to think I am anything but what I am. No one reads your letters so how about giving out with some of the dope I want. Please Del. It doesn't matter to much but I do want to know.

Lindy wrote and he said some nice things about you. Said you were sweet and very pretty. That he liked you and didn't want me handing you a line. You understand he considers me a good hand at that. Said you were worth all the girls I knew. That is his stamp of approval baby, so you won him over and I don't know how. He always seems to find fault with girls I get a crush on. I think he is in favor of you getting the brand on me so I will have to step easy from here out. Bet you told him the things I write to you. You are a card for doing that. Trying to swing everything your way and that isn't fair or is it. They say all is fair in love and war. Sometimes I wonder if that isn't true.

We were in the campaign at Okinawa. The old ship got a few glory bars to her credit now. We fished a jap pilot out of the drink. Saved his life I guess but I doubt if they would do the same for our boys. That is war though. No use of killing more than we have to although at times I do wish they were all dead. They sure haven't treated our prisoners of war with any amount of decency. Guess thing in Europe is about over with Hitler dead. Be home *J.E. Campbell MM1/C* to stay one of these days and won't that be nice.

I should be able to get myself a fair enough job some place. Get the car that I want and an apartment or small house in a little town somewhere there in the East. You would like that wouldn't you Del. Going to get a bed big enough so I won't never have my feet over the ends. After six years on this rack I have, well that seems important. Then you are getting a chance to fit right in with that, honey. Do you like the idea? We could make that bed big enough for two. I know what I want. Do you or is that question to personal?

So, you are curious about that book I mentioned. Well now isn't the type of stuff that school teachers recommend for girls but it is hot stuff, sweet. We get all the top sellers out here and I dig in on most of them. Going to give me your opinion of that one or keep your thoughts to yourself. Must have been some days then. I think "King's Row" was better. Saw that picture and it was tops. One of the best going.

Del, you mention things you couldn't tell me in your letter. Look now I am in a long time gone. This war is cheating me out of part of my life. If there are things in your head let's give out to me. Honest I love you and it isn't much else I can say out here. I don't want to come home and find things aren't the way I have been thinking they are. I told you things. You must know by now just about what to expect. Let's don't build up something and have it fall through. You tell me straight and you get it that way.

Guess you think these last few letters are books. Give me something to work on and they stay that way. Going to sign off for now and I will be taking you along with me so don't forget. Your memories Del and my plans. I love you, darling, and always will. No ocean can keep me away too long. Just stay and remember you are mine and I will be wanting some loving when I get home. Bye now and happy dreams.

Love,

John

J.E. Campbell MM1/C

May 18, 1945

Hello Del,

Been letting you down the past two weeks, honey but I just couldn't seem to get any mood for writing letter. There hasn't been any mail either so I didn't have much to work on. The going gets tough for me at times and I get pretty well fed up with everything. Then I think about the happy days ahead when I can be home again and have you around and things get some brighter. Maybe I don't do so well at this letter writing. It is a job to get over points to you and this long-range romancing isn't so good is it? Bet we would be a lot farther along if I could get home some. Been a long time hasn't it, sweet? And do you remember that we wasted some of the days we could have had?

Yesterday was my birthday. Twenty-seven and I feel every day of it. You never tell me when your birthday is. How tall you are or just how much you weigh. Got my ideas of course but why don't you get some exact figures. I know so little about you and you do seem so important. You never mention things you do or what you want. Del I don't give out with that line about are you the type for a little cottage and all that go with that. You want facts baby and you get them. I got you pretty well figured and I won't miss far. Better send me the ring size though. It is a long ways between *J.E. Campbell MM1/C* here and home. That is a hint, honey. Be more definite and ask you if you want a ring now or shall we wait. I guess I am sure but maybe you aren't. You are just about all I have to think about out here and sometimes I wonder if you would approve of the way my thoughts run. Guess I better hadn't tell you the things I think about. I have too much sea duty to be having innocent dreams.

Guess school days are just about out for you now. I can just picture you having fun this summer. Wouldn't it be nice if we could spend a few days there at the old state park when it gets in swing. There are thousands of caves and places to explore. A nice stream for trout fishing and it is just about heaven for a war weary guy. How about some pictures from you this summer. The ones I have don't change you know. They just get scarred and old from handling. Big morale builder and I like every picture you send. One of them will always be my favorite. It couldn't be better and honey you are cute.

State side news just came in. Lots of good dope in the air these days. The war over in Europe and all of our forces turned loose on the Japs. They put out the dope on one of our big carriers. Almost one thousand men dead and a few hundred more wounded so you can see the war isn't over out here yet. If I get by this trip then it might be my last one out here. I *J.E. Campbell MM1/C* might get a lucky break and a school or something. Anyway, I don't see how it can last too much longer.

Don't think you know Gordon Lewis. He is one of my old school pals. Lt in the Army out here and has over three years in the Pacific without going home. Married a girl in Australia when he was stationed there and he is in the Philippines now. Wrote the letter to me from the front. Guys like that we owe a lot to. He said it is rough going and his campaign was getting a lot of Japs but had lost more themselves. No one in America can understand the ordeal those boys go through. There is no fun or glory in war. The dead and wounded can't be replaced and the sorrow to America should be our insurance against a future war.

Getting a gripe about keeping this damn light on honey so I will have to sign off. Sleepy anyway and I will try to write again soon. So, bye now sweet and remember I love you always.

Yours,

John

J.E. Campbell MM1/C

May 20, 1945

On the photo:

"She is the sea going baby that will bring me home to you. Love, John."

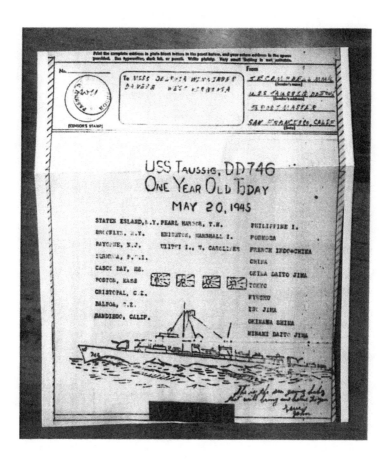

May 22, 1945

Hello Sweet,

Guess you know those letters from you keep getting through this way. Three in the last mail and that helps out. I don't think I can ever figure you out, honey but you can forget about any chance of me letting you down when I get home. Not one little chance in a million. No girl has ever lasted long before. I would just get tired of their line and get tired of writing and that is the way it ended. I don't find it tough writing to you and your letters are all tops. Del, I am sure you are the girl I want. Damn if only this war was over.

Gosh, I don't know where you heard any rumor that I would be getting a discharge. Absurd idea, baby because I am sure that I will be out here until these sons of heaven are blasted from their island home. They still have me wearing that tag that always spells sea duty. I have destroyer experience. Still young and the navy thinks well trained. Isn't easy to replace top P.O. They don't have so many in excess and we can't expect anyone to take the chance of ruining a ship for lack of operating personnel that don't know their job. I don't think the navy will discharge many men until the war is over. Too bad you had to pick a sailor. Do you think I am worth waiting for sweetheart? After all, with *J.E. Campbell MM1/C* with these young soldiers getting home I shouldn't think you would get lonesome.

Got two letters from Ken. The first since he was home and he sure gave you a buildup. Looks like my folks like my girlfriend. Anyway, I believe they want me to get settled and I suppose they figure some girl would be the thing to keep me home. Ken is still young and I don't believe way serious about any girl. The Kid has funny ideas about life in general. I never had any such idea and the navy sure hasn't improved my thinking any.

Don't have much to say about this D.O.W. stuff. There has been much talk about double time credit for sea-duty since the war and I have well over six years now. Double time would up that plenty and though I plan on leaving the navy there is always the chance that something like that might cause me to stay. The navy isn't tough for top P.O. in peace time if a guy wants to live under military rule. There will be plenty of travel but I think I have had enough. Expect you will have a lot to say about what I do anyway. Until I find out more dope, I am not going to sign anything. Got to stay out here anyway so it doesn't make much difference.

Del, I would like to have some new pictures. The ones I have are getting old. Gosh, *J.E. Campbell MM1/C* sometimes you write just as if you expect me to drop out of your life. Just as if you don't believe anything I say and a thousand times you have been told that I am not trying to hand you a line. You seem to think I have a million girlfriends. Silly idea baby. You don't realize how much time I have spent away from the states in the past five years. Then when we were in state side ports it was only for a few days. Didn't have much of a chance to meet the type of girl that a fellow really thinks about. You won't have to worry about me getting restless and pulling out on you. If I come home there I will stay and I do believe that no girl would find me much trouble. I have seen enough of the world and life. West Virginia seems a million miles away. Some place I dreamed up and even there at home some people don't try to get along. I don't like cheats and liars. If you ever lie to me Del, well guess I better hadn't think about that.

Well honey, guess this is just about finished for today. Takes a long time to get an answer back. I never remember much I say. Most of it isn't important anyway. Going to sign off for now so bye and don't forget I am always expecting your letters. Should they slow up now I wouldn't like it. Be good honey and I love you. (No fooling)

Always,

John

J.E. Campbell MM1/C

USS Taussig

New River Picture

May 30, 1945

Hello Honey,

No letters from you in the last mail and damn if that helps any. Can't seem to figure on anything these days. I like to think you write and yet there is no way of knowing for a week or so. Guess you never figured we don't get our mail every day. Maybe every ten days if we are lucky and that is good service. I can remember times when it was three months that was at the start of the war + I didn't have you writing me letters. I don't want you to slow up now. We have time out here and I am thinking it shouldn't be long before I get home again. The news is still all in our favor. Those B-29 are giving the Jap homeland a working over and with the boys from Europe on their way out here things have started to really roll. We don't expect a fast victory but there is no doubt that we will win. Even the Japs admit their problem is serious. There is a chance that Japan might give up. The fellows out here don't think so, but we only know the war side of the issue. Maybe their government at home can't hold out so well.

Guess it is nice summer days there now and this should find the laurel ready to bloom. That is the old home state pride + joy. Been a long time since I was there at this time of the year. Just happen to think today is Memorial Day. Funny how those things slip by out here. Bet you find plenty of fun at the park now. Should be nice for a swim and how I would like to try some of those trout up there. Jean said she is going to fish this summer. Bet she don't catch anything but a bad cold. Some pest around now so don't mind if this is a little fouled up.

Folks wrote that my old school pal, John Carte, is home on leave now. He should have enough points to get out under the system the army has in use. He went in on the north African invasion and into

Italy. Been there a long time and I believe he should get out. Lucky enough to have a wife and baby so that will help him out. I figure he has enough + I hope he makes it. Lindy wrote that some more of the gang we knew had been killed in Europe and Zickafoose is missing out here. Guys I have known for years. Sometimes I wonder how all this can happen. Seems like a bad dream or something and yet those facts are hard + true. *J.E. Campbell MM1/C*

Say Del, are you going to be away from home any this summer. Those work ideas cheated us out of a few days last time or do you remember. That last day I was home was the tops of any day I can remember. Honey, are you like that with all guys or was that a little special for me? You know people talk a lot and I know all about your recent romance. Hope you are having fun. I don't blame you any for going on dates. It would be way foolish for you not to but it isn't so nice for me to think about some other guy having all the fun with you. I know you are not serious with them but anything could happen. I am a little jealous and selfish where you are concerned. You are mine Del, and I want you to stay that way. I don't want other guys getting ideas or designs on you. I love you sweet, and I have all the reason in the world to be jealous. It is a long way between here and home and all I have is your letters. Those guys get more and I don't think you can blame me for not liking it. Better not stumble baby for I don't intend to catch any rebounds. You know what you want now and I guess you can get it. Just don't try to cross-up a certain sailor for I know that guy very well. You wouldn't get away with it, baby even if you did try.

We pick up some state side music sometimes. Makes a guy realize how much of that stuff he does miss. Would like to have a Saturday night off to spend with a radio somewhere. Guess I wouldn't be satisfied with that though. Would probably want to drink and have a hot shot time. It has been such a long time since I have had any liberty. I have almost forgotten what a meal on the beach would be like. A few beers, a floor show and those things. Last year we were getting a few well-earned liberties in old New York. I was having the time of my life. Wonder what our fate holds for next year. Should see the states during that time. Remember when I told you how long I would be gone? I won't miss it far, sweet. Another month and it will be pushing a year. How much have you changed in that time. Would you still be a little scared, maybe? Memories and they are precious. Next time they will be more to remember and maybe there won't be any more trips out here for me.

Looks like this will have to be the sign off for today. Just can't seem to do much at writing. Sometimes I can't write letters for weeks. You must find these very dull at times. Anyway, I try and that should prove to you that I don't forget my baby. Bye now and be good, honey. Keep those fingers crossed. It is my good luck charm and I will be home to you someday.

Love,

John

J.E. Campbell MM1/C

June 5, 1945

Hello Honey,

I had just about given up hopes of you writing again and then three letters at once. You did a good job of reading me off and maybe some of the stuff I wrote in those letters was a little rough. Just gave you an idea how my mind travels though. If you think you can change my ideas then I am willing to let you try. If you won't go my way then maybe we will try your ideas. How about some dope on just how you have things planned out? I might be interested you know. About my girlfriends at home. I can't remember any of them taking much interest in my welfare. I dated a few of them at times. Before + after I came into the Navy. I can't remember getting to a very serious stage with any of them. Not even so far as writing letters so I can't see why you worry about anyone there.

If I get any leave then you can be sure that I will come home. It would be worth my time + money just to see the folks but nothing could stop me at a chance of seeing you. Ken said a year had changed you a lot. It will be a year soon now and Del, it isn't letters that makes me think of you. They only make me hold to the memories of something I didn't figure would interest me much. I don't get ideas about girls to fast. You were cute and too young for me to worry about when I came home from out here. I was pretty well fed up on everything and wasn't doing much of a job showing the folks that I appreciated being home. Don't think I didn't notice you the first day you stepped into my life. You got a going over, honey. I knew you from letters and people so I took a look for myself. You made an impression but honest no one could have told me then you could be such a heart-ache for me. I had an idea that some gal with pretty blue eyes and probably blonde would hold my number. Everyone is sometimes off and I know for sure I was. You had my number baby and you hold it still. It is yours to cash in on if you want. I wish I could be as sure of you as I am of myself. Don't get any silly ideas that any letters could sway me one way or another. Your letters are swell and I like them. You were nicer and I liked being there with you. I like the way your eyes open with surprise or a show of temper. The way you kiss honey and those arms that steal around my neck like I always dreamed about. There is a lot I couldn't know about you but give me time and I will find out. Yes, Del you can pin on that private property sign any time you care to and I promise you *J.E. Campbell MM1/C* that it couldn't be too soon for me. It has been ten months since I was out with a girl. Long time isn't it, sweet? Probably be a lot longer to. You see you don't have much worry about me getting away from you out here. There just isn't anything to go for and I hope that when we hit state side that I can step off this little lady with leave papers in my hand. Then you could tease and play all you care to and I will like it. How would you get along with me for all of about thirty days? That is day-dreaming but then I do expect that dream to come true. There is no telling when we will get back. Everyone hopes it will be soon and I don't think they would keep us away for a year more. I guess the Atlantic fleet transferred out here should cut down on the time a ship must stay out without an overhaul.

They are really giving the Japs a pasting from the air. The B-29 have been over the main-land almost every day for a month and even the Japs admit their damage have been heavy. Okinawa has been a big loss to them and from all dope our forces have it almost secure now. No one can tell when this will all end. It might be a few months and it may take two years or more. The navy won't discharge any men until it is over. Maybe some of the guys over 40 but the war being over in Germany just stepped up our demand for men. The fleet gets new ships every day. This is the naval war out here. The Pacific has been the place for most of our first line ships ever since the war started. Don't get any ideas about me getting out before it is over. I won't not even if I wanted to.

I don't know for sure just what I will do when they start sending us back to civilian life. The peace time navy won't be too good. I could stay in but I don't think I want to. Plan on getting a job in a power plant or as machinist in a navy yard. Alloy would be an ideal place and it is more home. Then I might try the navy yard at Mare Island, Calif. or Philadelphia. I like both places. California best but it is a long ways from home. I am saving my money now so I won't have to worry about where I eat for awhile after I get out. The mustering out pay will help and with a little luck I can have enough to live well for a year. That will give me time enough to get settled. Most of that is if you + I do make a go of our affair. Otherwise, I wouldn't worry about a job. I could get a job with Standard Oil and off to South America or Africa. Good Year Rubber would be the same so don't you see I have you figured in my plans for the future. There is no doubt as to what I want and with the breaks and you *J.E. Campbell MM1/C* I would have it. We can't be sure about anything so let's don't get ahead of our times. Anything can happen and might and that anything could change the world for you or I. All America is waiting. Some young people understand their affairs better than you and I. They probably had more time together. It is the old game of wait and sweetheart, I hope you don't get tired of me being away and figure someone else in your plans.

Guess you are enjoying some nice summer days there now. No school and all the week to yourself. I am not so sure I like the idea of you going out with some guy. A date maybe I wouldn't mind, but going with one guy spells trouble and I am afraid that I will be thrown out on a limb. Honey, I love you and I want you all for myself. If you go out with this guy then he gets to know you pretty well. It is a long ways out here and you might forget. Things happen on wild parties and young people just being together. You may as well know now that I don't trust anyone much no matter what you tell me in letters. I have seen to many guys played for suckers. I don't trust no guy with you so better take it easy and let's don't be playing around. It won't work out. I am jealous as hell but I won't come pleading to you. You step over the line with some other guy and I find out then we are finished. I will drop you off no matter how much it hurts. That is final Del and you know I won't be too easy to fool. I think I know what to expect when I get home and it had better be that way. This is a two-way affair you know. If you expect me to come home then you had better stay the nice girl I think you are. I think I make myself clear so now you can have your say. You going on dates I am sure I don't mind. Going out with a guy often, I don't. Is up to you honey so be careful how you decide or you might have a very troubled sailor left out here.

About that poem. It came out of Esquire Magazine and I thought it was cute. Didn't you expect me to notice? Well, I can tell you I did so go ahead and get mad. Nice too, and more points about why I forget about a blonde. Blushing honey. Gosh, how I would like to see you now. Anyway, they are going to stop mailing the magazine and I think it is damn mean of them. Guess you are tickled that I won't find anymore naughty poems to send you. Still, you can't stop me from remembering not even if you tried.

Guess I had better secure this before I get myself into more trouble. Bye honey and be a good girl and send more pictures of yourself. You are getting to be more of a heart-ache each day and that's no fooling. So long until next time.

Love,

John

J.E. Campbell MM1/C

June 10, 1945

Hello Del,

No rack time today so I guess I will try writing a few letters and get up on this out-going mail. Not much doing except more letters from you. Guess we will have a few movies and a lot of work for the next few days. Sure, hope we get some more mail. Getting out here pretty good now. Your last letter was May 19th and that is better than most of them.

Gosh! I don't know where you pick up all those rumors about when I will get home. This isn't my first trip out here and I told you not to expect us home in a few weeks because the navy just doesn't work that way. These ships were built to take a beating and they get it. When we have time out here now and I got an idea that we might get home by the new year. That is still a long way off so you might as well get set for the wait. Some of them get back if they are hit but I wouldn't want that to happen. Someone always gets hurt and the Japs send those bombs to whom it may concern. I don't care about any of this glory stuff. I just want to get home in one piece when this is over. I am sick of war and of being out here but I know that there is no hope of getting it over fast. We still have time to put in out here and I am no better than the other guys. It is ok by me to stay as long as they do. I don't like for anyone to tell you I will be home anyways soon. Honey, there isn't any use of trying to make day-dreams come true. American women and I guess all the people back there have been wishing this over. That don't win. We will do the winning out here by giving them more stuff than they can throw back. They are getting it now but all the way from Pearl Harbor to Okinawa are the little cusses that spell our cost. There will be more and I for one wish that people will think for us out here as a unit instead of one guy. I guess that I am more your concern than all of the other guys. Well, I am glad to have it that way but these other guys have a girlfriend also. Some of them have a wife and maybe children. Well just maybe I want those guys to think I am a good Joe. I can tell you now that men overseas don't have to much use for unions, strikes and the fellows at home that figure their jobs are too important to allow them to enter the service. Maybe I shouldn't tell you that stuff. Probably Lindy is about the only person that really knows how I feel and I doubt if he would tell you. We in the navy have it easy to what the marines and army troops that go ashore do. We stand a good chance at getting back. Then there are these kids that should still be in school. Guys as young as you are. Let's forget about this stuff and let time take care of all *J.E. Campbell MM1/C* these problems. They are too big for me to understand and I have been looking them over for several years.

Guess you are having fun now. No school and a lot of outdoor fun. would like to be there now for a little fishing and the old swimming pool. Why don't you take a visit with your folks? Even if I did get home those trains run both ways and you don't think I intend spending this next leave without you around. No dancing, Del. I just never cared to learn but if you want to be the teacher then maybe I might be an apt student. Want to give it a try, sweet? I expect you would have a rough time.

About those twin beds. Maybe some do have that idea but not me. How about you? Your letters are getting very interesting. Things you say make it much easier for me to write. Then I wasn't henning about anything. I told you straight out and I guess you didn't like the idea. They say a girl always has changes of mind and I guess maybe you could think different sometime. Anyway, you can't blame me for trying and I bet other guys do to. Skip it baby until I show up in person and then we will have all that out.

Del, I told you I didn't write to Anna Mae. That is over and no fooling. It never was serious. Just that we had fun together and she was a good kid. I know Lindy liked her and he didn't like other girls I went out with. Our ideas on life just didn't fit. She was Brooklyn all the way.

She wanted too much for nothing. Anyway, she figured I shouldn't drink and that I was to be just a good guy for her. Well, we didn't agree on anything much and that is the story. Honey, you are easy to sway my way. I mean we don't argue much. Those letters you write are tops and I guess I know when my number is up. I can't see why you should worry about any girl. If we agree on a few more things then I expect we are all set. What do you think?

Got two letters from a girl in the army. She is a nurse and the sister of my best pal. He is on a destroyer out here. Don't get any ideas now. I never met her but we have been exchanging letters for over two years. She is in India and that is a long way from home. Writes a lot of interesting things but said life was plenty tough for her. I guess those girls rate tops for they do a wonderful job there or any place where wounded and sick soldiers are to be cared for. She talks a lot about the Chinese. Said they were dirty rascals and I can bet they are. It is my experience for anyone but she won't like it if they keep her away from the states very long. We plan on a get together when we all get state side *J.E. Campbell MM1/C* again and I expect it will be some party.

I don't get what you mean that some letters are dull. Aren't all the letters I write about the same? There isn't much news and I don't have much to gab about. Just trying very hard to prove you are my girl and I don't like the idea of other guys taking up your time. Checking through my locker today and I guess your letters have taken up about all the excess space. Guess I will have to throw them overboard and start with the next mail. You don't do bad at keeping a guy's morale up. I didn't know how much letters could mean until you came along. Then you say I have you all mixed up. You have the advantage and you know it. You have what it takes to grab any guy and me. I just got to stand by and hope I can get a chance to grab you off.

I wasn't trying to picture myself as a salty sailor to you. Guys are all very much alike and they probably look your way just as I would. They have the same ideas to, except I guess they might not tell you about them like I do. I couldn't very well keep you out of my life. I don't want to, but I talk straight and even though you tell me off I think you like me that way. You are nice, honey. Nice to look at and easy to fall for. There are a million little things that spell just you. My-post war plans went to hell when you came along so why be hard on me? You give my way some and I will go yours. That way things should work out so think it over. These are ideas I have that no one could change. You have me figured out pretty well and you know what I want and what I expect when I get home. I never said you would think I should have my way but things could blow up if I don't. Let's forget that anyway. It gets worse and you don't like being told things. How did we ever get involved anyway? Me trying to break your heart? Don't be kidding me. You knew I wasn't giving out any line months ago. I love you Del, and as far as I am concerned that is all that matters.

Look, I will be writing you a book if I don't hold up somewhere. Just about time for me to go on watch anyway. Please don't never slow up with those letters. It would be worse than you think for if ever I want anything then it is you. Bye now honey and have a good time.

Love,

John

J.E. Campbell

June 16, 1945

Hello Del,

Here goes honey. The third time that I have started a letter to you and didn't get two finished. This one I will. I had been watching your letters close and then the dope always gets out here so I guess my dream castle is all torn up. You could at least come right out and say it was all in fun and let it go at that. I have been expecting this to happen all along because I couldn't see you going for a guy like me. Guess it is better all the way around. Maybe things weren't supposed to work out for us. Guess I just didn't rate anyone like you.

Why all the questions about does your letters just mean more mail and that I will forget you when I get back to the states? No, honey you were all off there. I am going to miss your letters and going to miss my dreams about you. I guess I didn't exactly fall in love with you at first. It doesn't work that way with guys who drift about a lot. Trying to make me think you doubt things I write won't help any. You just didn't care if they were true to begin with. All right you had some fun + so did I. Someday you won't get off so easy. There are guys that can take your heart apart and play the game with you just as you are doing with the fellows now.

Maybe some of my letters were nasty and a little rough. For that I will say I am sorry. Many of them were written when I was tired and a little sick of being out here. I didn't try to impress you with the fact that I am old at this game of war and have been about the world some. Some of it was written because the greater part of my life has been taken up by this stuff. I didn't figure you simple minded enough to listen to any glory stuff about service men. If you got the impression that I think myself above the average run of guys then thinks again, my sweet. No one owes me anything and I don't want sympathy.

You remember me telling you about those "Dear Johnny" letters. What was wrong with you? Were you afraid I might laugh at your masterpiece and did you really think it would hurt me terrible bad? You never can tell about what I might do but I don't find writing this letter a very funny job. There are many guys on here that wouldn't feel *J.E. Campbell MM1/C* the same way I do. It isn't nice to know your girlfriend is giving you the run-around. Must be much worse when the woman is your wife. It happens too, so I am glad that I don't have a wife to wonder about. Sure, they all get lonesome and don't have much fun. Wonder if they think we are having one hell of a good time.

Yes, we do get some wonderful liberty at times. The ship will give us two cans of beer and maybe we can buy some from some money-making shipmate for one dollar per can. That is cheap for beer out here. Then maybe we might get a look at some native whore once and while. A look would be all and about all most of the fellows want. Liberty wouldn't be over four hours and the damn place stinks with heat. Well, that is the good times I have been having. How do you make out, baby?

Then here are some more points I can't see through. When I was home on leave last year there was any number of service men's wives going about with the fellows that are left. Sure, the guys knew all the boys were having a tough time, but there the girl was going to have her fun with someone and why should they miss out? That fun was a nice little petting party and drinks that came from someone's allotment checks. Well, I don't care to have that little deal turn my way so what you say I just turn you over to those fellows and you can at best be honest with them. Maybe one of the groups might even be turned into a husband once the boys come home and take their one and only off the dating line. You know you are pretty enough to hook most any of them. They do pretty good on the money end and are a sure bet to stay home.

I don't see how you can figure W.Va. such a bad place. You seem to do very good there. I am sure a few weeks there would help me out a lot. I could go for a long rest and a little mountain dew. Then maybe there are still a few girls about that I might be able to date. Guess everyone is enjoying the state park this year. Should be a lot of visitors there. They were several last year and I had a swell time there.

Saw a good picture tonight. Swing Fever with Kay Keyser and his band. Pretty good and the news reel showed Iwo Jima. We like to get that stuff to. I guess the news *J.E. Campbell MM1/C* holds a lot of interest for everyone. Rough going out here the past year and still tougher stuff ahead.

Del, you know me well enough to know I don't pull punches. All this doesn't exactly say I will stop writing you. Any time you send a letter out this way then you will get an answer. I like writing to you but let's keep them on a friendly basis. Otherwise, someone gets their feeling hurt and I do pretty well at the use of words. I don't say you do anything you shouldn't. That I wouldn't know. I do know things aren't going my way and then anyway you don't like the way I want things. I don't trust people much and can't see why I should. The guys go out with you for a good time + I don't like it. Why keep saying all this? You and I know we are washed up so let's admit the facts and forget we were ever so silly to think there was anything to hold us in a romance. We differ too much and there you have the answer. I don't want a girl who thinks about my ideas are all wet. She will have to see my side of living and you said no to that. O.K. there is where we leave all this loving business off. I do want to see you when I get home. Will want to take you out some if it don't spoil your plans. I think we shall always be the best of friends and will always have fun together. Sorry I didn't come up to your ideas. Maybe I would have, could, I have set my life back a few years.

Guess I have said enough tonight. Please excuse this mess if it sounds a little harsh and don't try explaining. You can write if you care to. Your letters are appreciated. Just tell me about yourself and what goes there. Leave the boyfriend at home and I will do all possible to make my letters sound good. Bye now and until I hear from you again here is wishing you lots of luck and the best of everything.

Always,

John

J.E. Campbell

June 19, 1945

Hello Del,

Got a letter from you today and I am thinking I have been quite a heel for writing the last letter. At the time I was a little peeved and in a terrible mood. If I promise not to do that again, would you forgive me. Most of the time I wouldn't care enough to ask that of anyone but I couldn't stay angry with you. Your letters mean to much so please do me a big favor and keep writing.

Honey, I guess it is impossible for you to understand how I feel about you and I know. I like you more than any girl I have ever known but we can't take chances. Maybe things would work out perfect for us and then maybe it wouldn't. It is that old story, Del that you are too young for me. I make my decisions but I do take advice. Friends of mine that are married say to go easy. They know more about two people being together all the time than you or I could know.

Suppose I be frank with you and give out with some points. More than likely, I would get married to most any girl I like and you would go easy there. No, I won't want to wait around for my life is going away from me in a hurry now. I won't be looking for some girl that is just really nice like you. See honey I expect I know you well. No, I would rather be out with some girl that gets around and I wouldn't be holding things against her if she is the type I like. Del, I don't have the old-fashioned ideas and you do. I have seen life both ways and you haven't. You have your first on lots of things. That is why I say you shouldn't be holding that crush for a guy my age.

Gosh sweet, don't get angry at this but you are really being foolish. You really didn't think I was a guy to be hooked without trouble, did you? I liked you and had fun taking you out but don't think I would be the same when I came home again. I like my loving all the way and you aren't giving yet. So what you say we drop this all back on a friendship basis. You go out and find yourself a guy and I will get along with someone else once I get state side. We will be the best of friends always. I was and still am very fond of you but I couldn't let anyone change my ways. I like them, honey, and seeing as you don't then we might as well get this straightened out for once and all.

Do you know I was under the impression that you were a year older than you are. Gosh, how did Have I ever get mixed up with a baby like you? Yes, I did want measurements. Exact weight *J.E. Campbell MM1/C* and everything. Does it seem strange that I would? Gosh, I want to know a lot about you. Got a ship mate I want you to meet when we get home. He is going to like you and it might go double. Nice kid and he is only nineteen. There are hundreds you can grab for the asking. You are lovely, Del. No line honey for that is the truth. I don't think I could hold you, sweet. Am afraid to take the chance. I would be insane jealous and hard to get along with. At least I know myself and I know I won't spoil things for you. About the pictures. Don't forget I want a few this summer. Want to see how much that baby has grown. Why did you have to come into my life? Don't you know I didn't want you to one year ago. Been a pleasure though but it can't be for keeps. Del, let's don't get things mixed up again. This war isn't over for a long time so please see my side of the story to. I might have encouraged you some but really, I thought it would be all cooled down. Honey, believe me when I say I do love you but there is too much to gamble on and I just wouldn't let you take a chance. There are other guys more suited to you. I will tell you now that I don't have any girl that has entered the picture. You are the only one and why I don't make a terrible effort to hold you I just can't explain. I am getting nowhere fast with this stuff. Can't you just tell me what you think.

That will be enough of that. The V-mail letter I sent you was for the ships birthday and had the name of the places she had been. We didn't get a look at most of them but the newspapers back there ran it as headlines. Lucky lady this baby. Just maybe I will make it through and home for good. Everyone gets around in the service but most of them would much rather be home. I am sure I would for I am sick of the sea.

Del, please don't let these letters get you angry. I write what I think and a lot of it is for you to decide. I don't say we can't get together but you must know now that I try to give you only straight dope on just how I feel. I thought about a ring but guess it wouldn't go. Better forget that and I don't think you wanted it anyway. Just keep those letters coming out here to me and go ahead and have yourself a time. Maybe if you just won't change, I might try doing something about it. I have all to gain, not every guy can have a nice young girl like you to write to and certainly not one that tells him the sweet things you tell me. So, bye now sweetheart and be good.

As ever,

John

J.E. Campbell MM1/C

June 27, 1945

Hello Del,

I got a letter from you today so I guess you rate a little of my time. Sorry that I have made a chump of myself in a few of my letters but do try and understand why I write that way and let's drop that argument for once and all. I say I won't treat you that way again + it is about all I can do from out here.

I am afraid I won't get home this summer, honey. Seeing as how you can't surprise me with your plans then how about telling me about the things you had all fixed up? I might be interested. Matter of fact I am sure I want to know so why not give out and tell me? I had a few plans of my own but I didn't have much hopes of getting back anyway. I would like to spend a few days at the park there. Take in our state capital. Drink up some of the beer there and most of all be with you some. You could fit with most of my plans if you wanted to. You are stubborn though + I expect you have trouble anyway that all remains to be seen so let's deal in the present instead of the future.

Not much mail the past two weeks. Just a very few letters and most of them from you. I think you must be peeved also for you don't write as often as you did. Getting sure of yourself sweet or losing interest? Letters always fall off after we have been out here awhile. No one passes up that chance to live and I don't expect to figure much with anyone's plans while I am out here. Not much use to care for there. Isn't anything we can do about it anyway. I am afraid you hold the top hand right now but just wait until I get home and get my hands on you. Then it is going to be a different story. We will have lots of time to see just who does the teaching and baby I wouldn't mind taking a few lessons from you.

Getting this engine room all cleaned up for some inspection. Most of the work finished but the gang have been working hard. I had some pretty tough jobs this past week and I am glad they are finished. Getting some very good information and repair work and I hope to cash in on it after this is all over. Right now, my rating helps me plenty for I know the guys on down the line have a tougher job than I do. I came up the tough way myself and I know their problems. Just one more rate for me to get and I don't think I will ever *J.E. Campbell MM/C* make that. Might not stay in the navy now but should I get the next rating in a few more years it could sway me into a navy life.

Now what was that crack about wishing I didn't have a good time while you weren't around last Summer? You are a little imp for saying that. I bet you enjoyed yourself at Beckley and as I remember I did have a very good time. Maybe the girls weren't so nice as you but they weren't so shy either. I always had fun at home. Some of the girls there I had known for years. Maybe I like the things they do and I wouldn't be surprised to find that I stand in well with a few of them. Good friends I know so don't figure that I won't make out there. I am no lady's man like some guys but I get along. You are having your good times now, aren't you? Some of the love affairs are very serious to, I understand. Better hadn't tease those guys to far or someday you will find that you, yourself, have gone past the teasing stage. I guess you know that I am not living a life of ease. Therefore, when I come home, I will be doing my best to live a few years in a few weeks. Maybe you can handle me and then maybe not. I can tell you now that you will have to be changed from the girl I left. Not much but a little. Do you want the details?

I saw a swell picture a few nights ago. "Since You Went Away". It was tops and tonight we have "Here Comes the Waves". Should be good and I'm not going to miss it. Haven't got any good books recently. Not too much time to read anyway. Did you give up on "Forever Amber" or just don't want to admit it was good stuff? I figured you should be a big girl by now but the way you tell me off about some things I have begun to wonder. I am not a dope honey, and you aren't the first girl I have known. Don't try telling me what to do because it won't work. If these letters get too rugged for you then we will knock them off. There isn't any use of me having you as a girlfriend if I can't have some fun. let's don't argue about that again. We never get things settled anyway.

Gosh, I thought you were going to send some new pictures. Other guys come first or didn't they suit you? Just where did you see a picture of the '38 class? I have most of that stuff at home. Why don't you take a look at my things sometime. Nothing personal there and you might find some of it fun.

Look Del this is going to be all for tonight. I will write you again soon so bye now and best of luck.

Love,

John

J.E. Campbell MMM/C

July 6, 1945

Hello Del,

This will make about three attempts at writing to you. I don't know what has happened recently but I just can't seem to click on anything with you. Your letters just haven't been getting out here at the right time and then maybe they don't tell me what I want to know. Honey, you don't let them get very personal. Doesn't it ever occur to you that I want details? The dope on things you are doing and plan to do. It is all important with me and about the only way we can keep these letters up. I don't expect to get home soon. There is plenty to do out here. We are drifting more apart every month + I warn you now that soon we won't be thinking the same as we did a few months ago.

Del, I love you and I don't want to miss on a chance to prove that. These last letters I wrote were a bluff mostly. Trying to see what you will do + I guess you are plenty angry. I don't mind that for it is fun getting you that way. I can tell when your temper is aroused and you are almost serious then. Why did I ever get mixed up with anyone like you? I guess I have always wanted someone but right now you are a big problem and most of it I can't solve. You will be so nice but I know I have a long way to go yet.

I think I shall buy some war bonds tomorrow. Have some money I want to get off my hands and that is one place to put it. I won't get many though for once this war is over, they will stop cashing them in and I won't have enough money ahead to allow any cash to be tied up. I have saved this trip. Paid off all my debts and have almost a thousand dollars to the good. At the rate I am going now that goes up one hundred a month so I won't have to worry about leave money once I get state side.

I figure the ring is out right now or really Del do you want one? It has got to mean something to you or there isn't any sense of buying one. Suppose I ask you to marry me next leave? Would that be a go or not? You have lot of time and a big field to pick from. Maybe I shouldn't ask you things like this now, but then I have the impression you could say just how you feel now. I am sure you know and honey I won't wait around much longer. It is a big gamble at the best. More than you realize now for there is a big difference in the way we have lived. Maybe there would be children and maybe not. Just maybe on all the things so be careful what you say and answer to all this. Once you make the first step it is hard to break away. Guys think twice before they *J.E. Campbell MM1/C* get serious with a woman who has been married. Girls don't seem to mind a man having had a wife before. You don't think those things could happen to you but they can. It is two people like you + I that trouble seems to follow. We might be the best ever and there it could be just our fate not to get along. Did you ever ask your mother about these things? She could give you a lot of points both ways and even I would be willing to listen. She knows her daughter pretty well if I am much of a judge, you have many of her points. What you say we listen to her and we could settle a lot of things? She must know by now that this is more than being good friends. Maybe she doesn't approve of me. I doubt if your dad would and don't tell me they don't matter. They do an awful lot so please let's don't go too far without them knowing.

Gosh, the news sounds great these days. There are plenty of people who think Japan will fold up soon now and things are rolling in the Pacific for sure. I think it will take time and a lot of men but they are finished. It is up to them from here out. Maybe they will decide to save a part of their industry in their cities by giving up. The Japs aren't so dumb and now that Germany is out of the war they stand alone against the greatest fighting force ever assembled.

Got some baseball news today and last year at this time we were thinking about New York and home. Don't you wish I could have those twelve days over? Things would be different wouldn't they baby? Well anyway, my favorite team isn't doing too bad and I envy the thousands of people that see them play every day. We get a few good programs beside the news. Some of my favorite songs came in on one program today and now + then we pick up the sweetheart of all the armed forces Dinah Shore. She is really great. Still, I would rather be home with you and listen to some hill-billy over W.L.W. or W.N.C. They are fun and you are any sailor's dream. I guess I have told you before that I think you have most everything and honey I sure hope you take a fancy to using that most everything on me.

It is getting dark topside now so I am going to sign off for tonight. Sure, hope we get some mail soon for you have me worried. Bye now sweet and have yourself some fun. Bet there was plenty doing July 4th. Let's give out with some long letters from your end and above all don't never let me give up loving you.

Always,

John

J.E. Campbell MM1/C

July 10, 1945

Hello Del,

Got two letters from you and that is doing good. I had begun to think you were going to stop writing. I like the snap shot, honey. Gosh, but you are cute now. Not much good that does me out here though. Sometimes I wonder just how much longer this can last. Maybe we are on the last lap now and even if we are it will still be some time before the navy turns anyone back to civilian life. There just isn't any use of thinking about anything for the future. We can't be certain of anything yet.

Bet you are having fun there now. The park should be nice now. It was last year at this time. I would like to try teaching you swimming but honest I am not so hot myself. If you can't do much swimming then try having a snap-shot of yourself in the new suit and let's see how I like that. Guess I would approve and at least I won't faint. I am sure I won't be home this summer. We couldn't make it now I know. I would like to get home in the fall of the year. Hunting season and football games. The best time of the year to have fun. Would you like hunting with me? I used to do pretty good but then there wasn't anyone like you about to keep my mind off the game I was out to kill. Was great fun and would be a good thing to rest me up from this stuff out here.

Got a letter from one of the guys transferred back in May. He is home now with 35 days leave. Lucky fellow but he is nice enough to let us know how things go back there. Gave us the dope we like to know about. Leave and ration of drinks and that stuff. Then some dope on state side girls. Going to the East Coast for a new assignment. Sure, could use something like that but I don't never seem to be the lucky one. *J.E. Campbell MM1/C*

I don't know why I talk about luck. I am always lucky or I wouldn't have you to write to. I will never understand what I did to attract your attention. Whatever it was I am glad it went over and I hope it sticks. Del, you would be surprised at the little things about home I do remember. It is hard to realize how service men and women are starved for the simple things that only a family home has. The food mother cooks up or a drink dad might have. A game of cards with Dad or Lindy and the afternoon fishing with Bill. Those are the things I came home for and then a bomb-shell got in my way and I found you were nice to have around. That is something I want to come back for this time. How many times have I remembered the first kiss and the last one? They didn't seem important then. I didn't even dream you could have so many of the points I like. It didn't seem possible that anyone so shy and young as you would cause me any moments of thought. You were sweet and those eyes do tricks to me across the miles. They are your stand out and they amuse me at times. Don't think I passed up other points. I didn't so don't worry. Got a pretty good picture of you all framed up in my mind.

Got a letter from Ken a few days ago. He seems to like the hospital there and just maybe he will never get overseas duty. I hope he doesn't for there isn't anything to this glory stuff and Ken don't need any of it. He has a good idea of what goes on out here by having wounded men to care for there. He is young and I would rather his idea of life weren't changed just yet. They will in time but out here it wouldn't take but a few months to bring him home a sullen and disgusted young man.

I guess you see Bill often. He just never writes but I expect he is very busy now. I think he could find time to answer a letter sometime. Maybe they think mail isn't so important to us. If only they knew what a *J.E. Campbell MM1/C* few letters does mean.

Say how are you at driving a car now? I can kick myself for not trying before I came in the navy. if you could drive, we could get sisters car and there are a million places we could go and not depend on other people to be along. This time I want to go places with you alone, and we are going to get along swell. I think you will fall in with my ideas, honey. You just have to or we won't never work anything out. Don't worry about what I will expect. I don't think you will mind. Most girls wouldn't and you couldn't be in a class by yourself. I just happen to like you better that is all so let's wait until I get home before you decide if we will agree or not.

I read in a sea navy magazine the story on the last ship I was on. She got hit at Saipan the trip after I was transferred and I guess they had a rough time. A lot of the fellows were hurt bad and several killed. Damn, these Japs anyway. I was plenty lucky to be off that ship. They were a swell bunch of guys.

Say, do they have a bus on the Rainelle route now? That must be O.K. You seem to be spending plenty of your time down there now. Sister will be telling me about seeing you. I think she likes you pretty well but don't let her know you have ideas for her sailor brother. She does a pretty good job at keeping me squared away and I listen to her a lot. Lindy writes sometimes but he seems to be very busy having a good time.

This is going to be all for today. I do try writing often but sometimes I tear the letters up. Anyway, honey you know I love you and always will. I will be home again soon and we will settle a lot of things then. Bye now and you are still my baby.

Love,

John

J.E. Campbell MM1/C

July 16, 1945

Hello Del,

No letters from you but there hasn't been any mail so I will try writing anyway. Not a lot to write about. The news sound great but there is no telling how long we will be out here trying to blast these nips out. Things won't be so simple as news reports would have people believe. These Japs are tough and no one can say different. Okinawa cost us plenty in men + material. The air attacks there were heavy and dangerous. They will be from here on so cross your fingers honey and just hope I stay where they ain't.

Guess you are having lots of fun now. Would be swell to be home. Just about this time last year I was enjoying the best leave I have had since I came into the navy. I guess it would be even better now. You would be along more. The places won't change much. I like the time I had to swim and wonder about up in the caves there. Bet you never thought I would be doing that but I did. I had a grand time + a swell rest. It would do me more good now than anything I can think up.

Say are the boy's home from Europe now? You never mention any of them. They are my old friends' baby, so even if you do sneak a date with some of those guys how about the dope on how they are doing? I expect you to be on demand. No soldier or sailor is going to pass you up and that's the way I like it. You don't think I want something other guys wouldn't have? You *J.E. Campbell MM1/C* are pretty much a dream girl sweet + I don't like being away from you. Someone could cause you to change your mind about your heart and I am not going to like any dealings like that. You are my post war plans and I am going to pin on a private property sign first thing when I get home.

Got a letter from Ken. Still got his home romance going by the mail route. He is some guy but I don't think any girl will give him ideas yet. He is too young to get serious. There is school ahead for him and a lot of life before any girl starts to rope him in. He is smart + not so little to make mistakes. Those two wouldn't get along. She has too much temper and not enough good horse-sense for him. She might be your best friend but I still have my right of an opinion and I happen to know the family very well. Even Pug has her share of the stubborn streak but I think she is tops.

Ever get your mind set on those twin beds or am I getting too personal? You never know what I might think up out here. Anyway, I think it would be much nicer with just one. That is the way I would want it. You would be closer that way. Don't mind me saying these things. It is still long-distance stuff and I can't read your expressions. I wonder just how free we will feel with all these letters behind when I come home. Just how far along are we and how much do we understand about what the two of us want? It could be so simple and then again, we might fight all the time. We are going to know for sure, honey. There are no old fashion ideas for *J.E. Campbell MM1/C* me. We can talk and plan and we will know if this is the right way. If we fit there will be no doubt and if our ideas cross then we will know that it has been nice just having fun together this long. You are going to know a lot about me and about life than you don't know now. I don't pull punches and you will have to listen. Some of it you won't like and our future hangs in the balance. You are fine now to do as you wish and you will still be then. Just don't let me hear you say I am still a nice guy after we have our say or I am afraid I will be a married man. That is hinting rather strong but you are for me if I can get you Del and I think you know that. It drives me silly just thinking about the nice girl, you are and the way you must think about how people should live. Would it seem silly if I said all I can think of is you in my arms? You to love and play along with. Those things seem impossible for me. All I have is the hope you send in letters and as time wares out here that seems to fade. Maybe there is someone else for you and maybe it is better that way. Then I will go on living as I have before. Taking out any girl that I can and getting along just anyway they care to.

Look honey, this letter is terrible. I guess they all are but I will write you again soon. You just keep thinking I am an O.K. guy and I will try to prove you right someday. Bye now sweet + happy dreams. Thanks for all the swell letters and how about a kiss by mail. So long and be good.

Always,

John

J.E. Campbell MM1/C

July 21, 1945

Hello Del,

Two letters from you today and thanks, honey. I have learned how much letters can mean to a guy since you started sending them my way. Things are going along swell out here. The navy getting head-line news and the guys getting very homesick. They are hitting the nips hard these days and there is plenty chance that the Jap government will try for peace terms. They know they are through now and they use the works at Okinawa. The mainland will be invaded next and if the Japs are smart, they will quit now. Just maybe, baby so don't get your hopes up.

So, my letters make you mad at times? Don't you like for me to think you are nice? I like you Del and don't mind saying so. You don't expect me not to notice your figure do you? It isn't my fault if you stand out in a class by yourself. I know you can use your looks to hook almost any guy you want for all the fellows fall when a pretty young thing starts showing them favors. Well, I am no different from the rest except maybe I don't trust so much and, don't have the same ideas about love making and those things. I live my way honey and not even you will change that. You more than have my ideas figured out. You have just almost told me they were wrong. Maybe so sweet but I won't be going out with you long if I can't change your mind. You are set on giving it a try, aren't you? That is ok by me. Just don't expect me to promise to go your way. We will be on trial and you have my number. Just cool down and it will be my deal. That is the way it is, sweetheart. You have your choice so if you don't like my language then start hunting elsewhere. You will find it lots of fun and some guys are stupid enough to think girls just have to be perfect. I hope it is ok for me to say I don't expect a girl not to have fun. If you are old fashioned enough to believe things I like are all wet then we wouldn't fit anyway. Why be so secret about the things you are thinking? I am just one guy and not a news-paper you are writing to. No one else knows what you write in these letters. You hint to much Del and don't say what you mean. Gosh, honey I will tell you straight. Can't you do the same? After all I can't see you blush all the way out here and it is better for us both to know just how we are thinking about our lives. *J.E. Campbell MM1/C*

You ask about Anna Mae and I will tell you again that we are finished. Yes, I did like her very much. She is all the big town and is a very lively girl. We differed on too many things and argued too much. It was never anything but a great friendship. She likes to tease the limit and then I guess she liked me some. I saw her twice in New York. Once on a date and once when she just happened to see me on Broadway. There were a lot of points she had that I liked. There was nothing shy or reserve about her. Does that answer your question and satisfy you or should I go into details more? I think you are a bit jealous, Del. Really now you didn't expect to be the first girl in my life, did you?

Now to answer your question about others. The army nurse happens to be just a pen pal. The Sister of my best friend and her home is the New Jersey state. She writes the most interesting letters of anyone I know and I was writing to her long before you arrived on the scene. I admire the courage of any girl that is in the service and I have a great respect for the nurse's village is in India. Up where the going is tough. Just maybe letters from + to me takes up some of her time and if so, I am glad for after being out here I know how to appreciate mail. I write to the wave in New York some. She is ok and nothing to worry you. I am not her idea. That is them all. No girls at home on the side. It was mostly your fault I went out with Frankie last year. Honey, I don't like to be "stood up" on a date and you don't know just how close you came to being a closed chapter in my life over that little deal. You didn't need to make the crack about did I find her a nice time. Ok she didn't mind showing a guy some fun. Frankie will do well for herself. I wouldn't have had any trouble getting her again but I didn't because of you. No, I didn't think she is as nice as you are. I told you before you got points, I have been looking for. I like your brand of kissing and well – I just like you. Will you please stop being a little imp by asking me silly questions? When I get ahold of you my heart beat steps up. You are what I want and I will get you if I can. Satisfied now or is that plain enough?

Think you are wrong about my favorite magazine. We got a copy today. What's wrong, honey. Afraid for me to look at pin up girls? Well, the sailors like them. There are a lot of them pinned up about the ship. That is America honey and to hell with the old bags that want to stop the magazine. These guys out here aren't kids. So, what if the pictures are vulgar *J.E. Campbell MM1/C* in the opinion of a guy in the Senate. He is back state side where he can look at the real ones. We are out here where we get the pictures some guy draws. Now I know they are scantly clad but what do you think we want. Something in skirts from the old days. No, Del the boys like a show and it is ok by us if he draws them all in their birthday-suit. Now go take a good look at my picture and blow your top if that will help you any. Pretty soon you will be telling me that I have to face the bulkhead (wall to your landlubbers) when you get yourself ready for a night's sleep just because that picture and I might be getting naughty ideas. All I can say is that picture is more luck than the guy. I never get in on anything like that.

Macy and Lindy, both mentioned you in their letters. They are swell people and the little lady made a hit there. Really Del they like you. They sent me two cakes. Haven't eaten them yet but probably try them out tonight on the mid-watch. I guess Darrell will be home soon and Sister will be very glad to have him back. Lindy is all for the guys out here. If I didn't understand him so well, I might let up at times but I do my best just to make an impression for him.

I hope you get those swims in this summer. You will make an eyeful for the guys to watch anyway. We are starting on our twelfth month out here. Now we can hope with a little more reasoning for some state side time. Gosh those long-awaited days. Sure, it is going to be nice to see you again. Maybe you will be at the station honey and stand by if you are. Like to get kissed and mugged in public. Well, that is what is in store for you so it is fair warning.

Just about to forget to tell you I was just ribbing you about the boy-friend. No one told me anything. You almost did make excuses though. Forget it honey. I love you and always will. I don't worry about other guys now. When I leave next time, I might. If they can get you now, they are lucky. If I get home they will be lucky to get you back without a private property sign tagged on. Bye now Del and please don't never stop writing. I live on those letters. Be good honey and have a good time.

Love,

John

J.E. Campbell MM1/C

July 29, 1945

Hello Del,

You will have to harden the paper honey, but it is all I have now. No letters from you the past few weeks but just maybe they haven't gotten up with us as yet. Then you could be a little peeved at some of the things I write but I can't see as that will do you much good. You have to write baby if you expect to get along and you will have to learn to like the way I write. Those things in letters are just the things I think about out here. I am not a civilian used to daily contact with girls, Del. They have been few and far between in my life and I guess I am plenty dumb when it comes to know *J.E. Campbell MM1/C* the ways to please a woman. I write what I think and if you can't take it then we may as well stop thinking about each other now.

The news looks good these days and still there might be a long time to go. The top command doesn't think so and the Japs put out peace feelers. The navy came out with a point system but hell, I don't have a chance. Anyway, I don't expect to get out until it is over. The fleet is getting into the news a lot these days. From the dope we get the boys from our carriers got most of the Jap fleet that was around the mainland. They couldn't have enough now to bring on a surface battle so landing operations won't be heckled by their fleet. Hell, why do I bother you with this damn war. It must be imprinted on my mind. *J.E. Campbell MM1/C*

Guess you are really enjoying some nice weather there now and plenty of time for a swim and lots of outdoor fun. This is the best time of the year in W.Va. Maybe not but it was lots of fun for me last year. Always my luck to get home in the winter where there isn't anything doing. Sure, hate to get home in zero weather when I have been in the tropics. I did that about three times and almost froze.

I got a letter from Ken. That guy is really getting in the groove. He is changing plenty and will be rough to handle when he gets home. He doesn't say too much about the girl at home. She will never go over with him. Ken isn't easy to fool and I don't think that girl is going to stick *J.E. Campbell MM1/C* to any one guy for long.

Say what is this dope that you want to be a nurse? I have other plans for you, Del. The nurses have been doing a great job. This war + their work will be heavy even after the fighting is over. A pretty girl like you would go over with the guys. I am thinking about taking up your next hundred years though so don't forget me in your plans.

Guess you are having yourself a time with that part of the army you said was sweet. Ok honey you rate your fun and you can but I am plenty jealous. That guy is getting the things I want. I hope you don't expect me to like that but there isn't much I can do from out here.

This is all for now so bye sweet + don't forget I love you and please keep writing.

Always,

John

J.E. Campbell MM1/C

August 5, 1945

Hello Baby,

Two letters from you last mail and that is nice even if you were a bit peeved at me. I am sorry if you are a bit mixed up because of my letters. Material for writing is hard to get and I do the best I can with what I have. There is one thing I can tell you for sure. I would be a bit foolish to feel sure of you out here. People change in a year and things happen. It wouldn't be hard for you to go sweet on some guy now and me being out here doesn't help my case any. No one can say I am losing interest. I think I write more now than ever and I am sure no girl ever got much attention from me while I was out of the states. I told you honey that I am making a play for you and it is straight. I know what I want and intend to get it so don't start to worry about how much I think about you out here. It is more often than I thought I would and sometimes I wonder why we can't get home. Damn, I am losing out on a lot of fun with you. I sure, would appreciate a chance of giving you some time to prove those things you put in letters. I had enough before to know it is nice but honey that is only the starting of what I want. We will get along. It is just the waiting that causes us trouble now.

I didn't know that Phylis and Imagean were home. They are nice and I like them. Phylis is tops as far as I am concerned. She + Harold really gave me a good time in Norfolk anytime I happened to get in there. I had some fun with Imagean last year while I was in pre-commission school. She is a good sport. I guess you got yourself a lot of dope from them. They know me very well and I wouldn't be a bit surprised at some things Phylis might tell you. She knows the navy and this sailor, and I guess any navy wife would understand us better than just any civilian.

Guess I do remember the old swimming hole just below our house. Many are the times we spent a few hours there. Bill + me with a few of our pals. It was sure some fun even if we did get cut up on the rocks and weren't very good at *J.E. Campbell MM1/C* swimming. I can just picture you at that place. Anyway, would like to be there with you. You couldn't drown me for the water isn't deep enough and I think I would be naughty enough to get my face slapped. I know I can't make it so why dream about those things? Even with the war going our way we still have some time to do out here.

Gosh, honey, you will be going back to school again soon. More worry for me because I know how some of those school day romances work out. With my old game it didn't go over but some of the others in the class it did. My best pal from school days was home recently. Lindy saw him. He was a great guy. Maybe the army will let him out. Has a wife + baby now and spent about three years in Italy. That is rough going for anyone. Lindy also said one guy was home from out here. He was on the carrier Bunker Hill. She took some bad hits and was sent back. She was a familiar figure in the carrier task force out here since early '43 and had a nice record.

You wanted to know if that school letter is mine. Yes, it is. Most of the things in that box are. Things I picked up in school and the navy. Some going over the line. Some pictures from Brazil and South Africa. I did have a grass skirt from Samoa but gave it away. Jean has one from Tsoba. A lot of swell memories and a great bunch of guys.

Honey, I didn't say your letters weren't appreciated. They are and I wish you would write more often. I don't have any gripe there though for you write more than I do. Sometimes I think it was your idea to get all this started but I don't object any. I love you Del, and just maybe someday you will believe that. Right now, you doubt anything I say. I don't doubt you. I think I know about how you feel. Sometimes I think I know life pretty well but even some innocent girl like you can make me very foolish. Well anyway it is fun trying. Going to sign off now sweet so bye and be good until I get home. Then maybe we can be a little more loving than ever and that will be my Pacific dreams come true.

Love,

John

J.E. Campbell MM1/C

August 11, 1945

Hello Honey,

Guess I may as well try writing you a letter. The guys have their hopes up over this peace offer but from late news reports we can't tell just what to expect. I don't think anyone could blame me for saying I hope the thing is over. With Russia in the war and this new bomb we have they can't expect to last much longer. This entry of Russia set us with them for sure. The fellows out here really think the Reds are tops and give them much credit in the war. They seem to be all for a world of peace and from the reports on this bomb everyone can be expected to be against another war. This new weapon can wipe out a city and with modern air-craft no nation can consider themselves out of bombing range. Enough of that stuff. Just thought you might be a little interested in how I feel about this. Honey, if I was a praying man I don't doubt but what I would try some of it here. I want to come home very bad. It is something I can't explain. There are days that this life out here goes against the will of any man. It affects us all and not one of us will forget. Every man on here would be happy to see this over and getting home again. It is all we have to hope for.

We haven't had any mail for a long time now. Not much fun missing out on the Uncle Sugar. That is our contact with home and it is my personal contact with you. Those letters seem to be in every mail and you have been swell at building up my morale. I think I know now why guys go to hell out here if their girlfriends let them down. I am a vet at this game, honey, and yet I am afraid I would be terrible disappointed if you should let me down now.

I have been thinking up a lot of things that I might do once I get home. I believe I can get a job at Alloy. They should have my line of work there. Five days a week and the pay isn't too bad. That place is a sure bet for good working conditions for a few years because of the work they produce. It is close to home too and I want that so I can have some time with the folks. Things won't be easy for me. I will have to learn how to be a civilian and right now I might be a little afraid of the big outside world. I am willing to try and I won't be exactly broke. I can have enough money to live awhile even if I don't get a job right away. Then should I decide on a few other things we could use some cash I guess. Guess by the time you get this your vacation days will be up *J.E. Campbell MM1/C* and maybe mine will have started. Too bad I had to miss out on all the fun this summer but let's make it a deal to make up for some of it next year. Okay by you or is my girlfriend still in doubt about the ideas of this sailor?

Just how much gossip did you pick up from the girls on their visit. I know women talk plenty and I don't doubt but what you were all ears. Did they tell you how much sailor I am honey or did they say I am a nice guy? I might be a little interested in what some of my friends think of me. I don't figure you are going to allow anyone to help you make up your mind about me. Wouldn't be surprised if you don't have your plans pretty well made out now. Well just be careful or I might try changing some of them. Serious baby, I don't think I will cause you much trouble. You are what I want and I am sure of that. I love you Del, and it would take a lot to change that. Still, you have your opinion and I can't be too sure of anything. Maybe it won't be long now before we can talk over these things and it won't take us long to sum up the differences in our lives.

Del, you always say you are just the same as when I left. Do you realize just how little I knew about you? I didn't ask many questions. Just took you as you were. Found you were very nice and easy to get along with. I was surprised at my interest in you and you couldn't know how my heart beats stepped up when I found you in my arms. That was about the best moments of my life and I will have to admit that I really didn't know how to act. I am sure that was the first time in a few years that I didn't start making passes. You are so young that I am still afraid this all isn't so. Sometimes I wonder what you would have said had I stepped out of line. Want to tell me or do I have to wait. You know next time I will get ideas don't you, Del? I guess you are getting used to guys now. Anyway, I am not home yet so we will still have some time to think over the things we want.

I hope you aren't bored by these letters. At the best they are one hell of an excuse of a letter to the girl I love. I never had to much experience at trying to please the opposite sex with pretty words so you will have to be satisfied with me as I am until you can change me to your way of living. I like you Del for the person you are. You made a hit with me and you hit hard. No matter when I get home, I want you for keeps so bye now honey and make a wish list for me that this damn war will be over soon. Best of luck to you and keep those letters coming out this way.

Love,

John

J. E. Campbell MM1/C

August 16, 1945

Hello Del,

Today has been a one that will make history. The President gave the official announcement that Japan has agreed to peace terms and our fleet hoisted the battle colors in symbol of victory. We can be proud of a job well done and there is no doubt but what Russia getting in the war and the new atomic bomb rushed the nips into yelling uncle. I am glad the yellow bastards are finished. They have been tough and may still cause some trouble but I think we have finished with them.

Guess everyone is very happy in the states now. Most of them will celebrate with fire water and really have a hell of a good time. I will save mine for that first liberty state side and I really expect to go on a binder then. It would be great fun to see the capital V-day parade though. Damn we miss all the good fun and free drinks.

I know there will be a million things you will want to know but there isn't anything I can tell you except I want to get home just as soon as possible. I don't know just how the navy will go about discharging men and I couldn't even guess when we will get to come home. They shouldn't keep us out here to long for it has been a year now and the ship has a lot of steaming hours. Maybe my luck will ride with me for once and I can get out when the ship comes home.

Del, I don't know what I will do when I get out. Guess I will come home first but I can't be sure of even that. I will have to get a job right off if I expect to make a go of civilian life. Maybe I will stay in West Virginia and then I might not. That depends on the work I can get there. The only reason I would stay is to be with the folks. Honey, that state stinks as a place to live but then a guy always has things at home to keep bringing him back to stay. I do have some money ahead but it won't last long. The paychecks will have to start right off if I expect to get anything to hold me out there.

Now here is some dope you aren't going to like. I will have to make sure that I am all set before I could think serious of any girl. I know that you have plenty of time but I am not so young anymore. I won't be home but a few days at the most. Crossing bridges now before I come to there but this is the way things will shape up. I will be off again for a job. Maybe somewhere close and I would be home weekends. Maybe out of the state and that would be just as bad as the navy as far as we are concerned. Then you will want to know about things I will be doing. I have missed out on a lot of fun the past six years. To say that I intend on making up for lost time is putting it about right. I like to drink some and sometimes I get damn drunk. Would like to get myself a car if I can and as for a girlfriend, I think I have one. You are so sweet Del, that I really don't know why I keep stringing you along. You aren't my type and you know it. I won't be satisfied with your kind of fun or at least I don't think I will. Now honey maybe this isn't just the right thing to say but you can't hold to your ideas forever. You have to figure my side of the story too or face the facts that I will be going out with other girls. That is up to you and you had better start thinking hard about it now. I am not going to double-cross you. I think you are everything I want but I am not a teen-age guy. I know what I want and I can get it. If you hold to your ideas on what our relations should be then someone else is going to get my attention. Think it over because I mean it and I don't want you to build yourself up to a big letdown when I get home. The girl I marry won't have to be innocent or perfect. Just someone I like to be with. Someone that likes my sort of fun. the guys you know don't figure women as I do. Hell, I doubt *J.E. Campbell MM1/C* if you see through all this but if I write it out any plainer the sensor would send the letter back. I think the age difference is just too much and that is our trouble. I don't know though for even when I was in high school I had about the same ideas. I guess that is why I thought I liked Freda Kisler. Freda likes living and she knew what she wanted from life. If I hadn't been such a goof this navy would never had spoil my chances there. In a way I am glad this happened for now you came along but honey you are a terrible head-ache. The sweetest most loving girl I have ever known but what good will that do me? Del, you have the stop sign on me for now. Some girls hold out until they are married but most don't. If you plan to I am not your guy and there you are. Take it or leave it sweet and please let me have some definite dope for California and Texas come before West Virginia from where I am now. I can assure you that I will do alright with someone else. This stuff is on the corny side but honey you can bet your scanties I mean every word of it. I talk straight. Take it or leave it stuff and I don't intend to play around with baby Del for a year or so. You are a big girl now and can say one way or the other. Do I get an answer or do you bypass me on this one too. You will be bailing mad before you get this far along so no fancy stuff to end this letter up. The war is over and before long I shall be a civilian + I live by my own creed. You like yourself as you are and I like my ideas. One of us will have to change a lot or both of us change some. I am a stubborn guy but could be handled some. The choice is yours. Make it and we will see how things go but for cripes sakes please don't play the innocent to me any longer. Sometimes your letters sound like a letter from a good sister of the church. Be lady like if you want to but hell, I am not a kid. Fill those letters up with stuff I want to know. Bye now honey and try to figure my angle along with yours.

Love,

John

J.E. Campbell MM1/C

August 18, 1945

Hell Honey,

Things happen fast these days but most of them are pleasant dreams now. Here is something that will interest you or I hope it does. I am being transferred. Heading home and out of the Navy. It will be a month or more before we get started back, but I should be home and a civilian by November. Lots of this seems like a dream now. The war over and a Navy points system to discharge men. I had enough points and a few over and then the dope came through to get us started home as soon as possible. Really, I didn't expect anything like this. It is great news for me. The first chance at being home for a long stay in seven years.

The navy gave out the names of the ships in the third fleet that were in on the final blow against Japan. This ship is a part of Task Force thirty-eight the most famous task force in any Navy and we didn't do bad for just one year of duty out of the states. I am glad it is over and we didn't have to invade the Jap mainland. It would have cost plenty in the lives of men.

This letter is going to be all mixed up. You can stop writing now. I wouldn't get your letters any more for I will beat them home. Been almost a month since we had any mail and I am far behind the dope on you. I guess we won't get mail before I get transferred. You can tell me about the things I missed out on in the last letter you wrote. It will be better that way, won't it?

Gosh, Del, I am all nervouss about this deal. Honey, I have got to click out there and you are going to help me. Maybe if you hadn't come along, I wouldn't be in any hurry to quit the Navy. It has its points in peace time but not enough to cause me to be away from you. I will get by and I know I can get a job but it will be a big change. I am used to the *J.E. Campbell MM1/C* Navy routine. A place where every move is planned and it is a part of me now. People out there don't talk my language. Maybe things will get dull and I will go on a binder. You will have to expect those things. Do remember this, Del? I am no kid and I don't like to be lectured. You can change me some but don't rush it. We have lived a lot different and on a lot of things we won't agree.

I wrote Sister and asked her to check on a job for me. I plan on trying Alloy and should find something there. Will be home for a few weeks anyway and I want to see a lot of you during that time. I guess we should have things straightened out before I go to work and know just about what we want to do. To rush things would be foolish. I plan to get married but not right away. The pay checks will have to be sure before I take that step. In the meantime, we will be together a lot. There are a million things to talk about and if things don't go right for us, I won't be able to get along so well. You know I have built my hopes around you. Please baby try not to let me down.

Hell, I can't write a letter today. I will write if we step along the way and it won't be too long after this year. You have something to plan and now so cross your fingers and stop all those romances you have going. I am your guy now and I don't want anyone else going around with my girl.

Guess you won't get the grass skirt. Maybe you won't care too much seeing as I am getting home. I will find something else for you. Going to sign off now, sweet. Bye now and save that loving for me. It has been a long time gone and you have a lot to make up. Be seeing you soon.

Love,

John

J.E. Campbell MM1/C

Sept. 7, 1945

Hello Honey,

Guess I had better write or you will begin to wonder if I am not lost along the way. We have been stuck on this Island for ten days just waiting for a ship going back to the states. It shouldn't be but a day or two more now and we should hit the West Coast by October 1. Left the ship on August 20th so you can see we aren't getting far. About fifteen hundred miles is all.

This isn't bad here. We get a few hours loading stores sometimes but just take things easy as the general rule. Get a few cans of beer each night and movies and U.S.O. shows. Some of the stage shows are pretty good. Girls from the states and they are damn nice to look at. Then we see some Amy + Navy nurses. Sea is all though so don't get any ideas, baby.

There isn't any dope on just how long it will take to get out once we hit the states but I expect to be home by Oct. 15th. Some say we get thirty days leave and report to the naval station near our home for final papers but no one seems to be certain. There is one thing I am sure of. They are putting on a high powered drive to keep the regulars and I hope I don't get tempted. I like the navy at times but I like being home + with you more.

There seems to be a million sea shells here on this Island and I bought a basket made from them to bring home. be willing to swap it up to you for about a thousand kisses if you are interested. These fellows stationed here spend lots of time on the stuff and I guess they pick up plenty of spare cash from the guys going state side. The stuff isn't too good but these shells can't be picked up just any place.

We haven't had any mail for almost two months and I really don't have any recent dope on you. I miss your letters Del, but I don't worry for I know you will be there when I get home. It is nerve wracking to have so many miles to go when I know that I am on my way. I know too little about women to understand you and I know I have a lot to learn. Honest Sweet, I have been ribbing you about a lot of things. Your romances and that stuff but seeing as I am going to be home soon how about letting those guys drift their own way now? I am just as jealous as any guy and I am not going to stand for other guys going out with you while I am there. It would cause trouble and gossip and, Sweetheart, I am tired. Very tired of people fighting and that stuff. There were days out here my life wasn't worth a plug nickel and now that is over. I want to forget about that stuff. Still these years haven't helped my temper any and I rage at times. You have a problem on your hands and maybe when thirty days are up, I will know if I stay home or go back to the fleet.

Do you think it silly to dream about people you   like? I mean day dreams and some night dreams too. Honest you appear at night now so often that I know for sure you are causing me to think about you too much. Different than a few months ago when you just came in smiling and left. Sometimes now you stay and I even get my hands on you at times. Last night it was trouble though and I will tell you about that sometime. Then one night you came in with more of yourself exposed than a lady should allow. Honey, when I dream of you like that it almost puts me in a mood for there is an empty space in my life and there never has been anyone in my life that I wanted like I want you. The days are just hell when they drag along with nothing to do. Your picture dances and teases me all the time. I wish I could forget and save us both some bad moments but I know now I will come home for a while because of you. You are too much of a lady for me Del. Your type never interested me for long but then I never knew anyone just like you. Fellows tell me I have to change some to make a go with you. Give some and you would do the same. It might be that they are right but I am so damned afraid that we just won't get together. Hell what am I talking about? We will get along as friends always. We have already agreed to that, haven't we?

With a little luck I will be home for a little fun during the hunting season and for some football too. With gas ration off a guy should have plenty of fun. maybe you can hunt with me some if you want to but then that might cause too many of the ladies there to say things. They always do where I am concerned and you are too sweet for me to cause any trouble to come your way. I don't believe in their old fashioned ways but you might. I think people should follow their own ideas and desires but I would have one hell of a time making you see my way.

They don't sensor my mail anymore. Guess I will have a lot of letters when I get home for, I know I have some back mail. Maybe I will write again and maybe not. All depends on what mood I am in I guess. I always like writing you but it can be over-dose and I don't know just how you answered my letters the past few months.

Del, I love you so much. You know that don't you? These days are waiting are terrible. I think of holding you in my arms and your lips and your smile. They haven't me honey and just for the hell of it I will tease you and stroke your hair and feel your arms as they tighten when you give those kisses back. I know you like it and so do I. We will fight a little, love a lot and baby if we have any chance at all we have a lot of happy days ahead. Maybe I will have to wait for you to grow a little more but I am willing. The waiting will be worthwhile and I am sure glad I waited until you came along. Bye now and be a good girl and I will be seeing you soon.

Love,

John

John Campbell's Service Statement

NAVPERS-601   CAMPBELL, John E.   9
NAME _____
    (Name in full, surname to left)

   265 87 39   Rate   MM1c   USN
(Service Number)
Date reported aboard _____ 5-20-44

     U.S.S. TAUSSIG (DD746)

     NTS NORFOLK VA
   (Ship or station received from)

<u>18 August 1944</u>: Commenced tour of duty
outside continental limits of U. S.

�

Authorized to wear American Area and
Asiatic-Pacific Campaign Ribbons in accordance with General Order No. 194.

<u>1 October 1944</u>: Crossed 180th Meridan
at Latitude 16° - 20'N.

Participated with credit as a member of
crew USS TAUSSIG (DD746) which was a unit
in Fast Carrier Task Forces, Pacific Fleet
(Task Forces 38 and 58) in the following
actions:

<u>5 November 1944 through 20 January 1945</u>:
Air strikes on Luzon Island, Philippine
Islands and Formosa in support of occu-
pation of Philippine Islands.

<u>12 January through 16 January 1945</u>:
Air strikes on Indo-China and China
(Hong Kong Area and Hainan Island).

<u>16-17 February 1945</u>: First Carrier based
air attack on Tokyo, Japan since 1942.

<u>20-22 February 1945</u>: Air strikes on Iwo
Jima, Nanpo Shoto in support of occupation.

<u>21 January and 1 March 1945</u>: Air strikes
on Okinawa Gunto, Nansei Shoto.

<u>2 March 1945</u> : Shore bombardment of Okino
Daito Jima.

<u>18-19 March 1945</u>: Air strikes on Kyushu
and Shikoku, Japan. While under heavy air
attack, TAUSSIG assisted in shooting down
two enemy planes.

J. A. ROBBINS
Commander, USN
Commanding Officer

NAVPERS—601

9

Name   CAMPBELL, John Emerson

265 87 39   Rate   MMlc

(Service Number)

Date reported aboard: 20 May 1944

U.S.S. TAUSSIG (DD746)

NTS NORFOLK, Va.

(Ship or station received from)

23 March 1945: Commenced air strikes on Okinawa Gunto in support of occupation.

6-7 April 1945: Underwent heavy air attack. Slightly damaged by near miss. Assisted in splashing one Jap plane.

15-16 April 1945: In twenty-five hours, ship off Amami Gunto, shot down 4 enemy planes unassisted (2 at night), assisted in destruction of 1 and turned 4 planes away from Task Group.

21 April 1945: Shore bombardment of Minami Daito Jima, Daito Shoto.

14 May 1945: Assisted in destruction of one Jap plane during air strike on Kyushu, Japan.

* * * * * * * * * * * * * *
* * * * * * * * * * * * * *

In accordance with ALNAV 64 of April 1945, is authorized to wear Philippine Liberation Ribbon with one bronze star.

J. A. ROBBINS
Commander, USN
Commanding Officer

NAV PERS-601   9

NAME   CAMPBELL, John Emerson
          (Name in full, surname to left)

   265 87 39   Rate MMlc USN

  (Service Number)

Date reported aboard   20 May 1944

     U.S.S. TAUSSIG (DD 746)

       NTS Norfolk, Virginia

  (Ship or station received from)

5 June 1945: Performed his duties in an
outstanding manner aboard the USS TAUSSIG
(DD 746) during a severe typhoon off Okinawa, Nansei Shoto.

Participated with credit as member of
crew U.S.S. TAUSSIG in company with Destroyer Squadron 61 during an attack on
an enemy convoy off Nojima Saki, Honshu,
Japan on night of 22-23 July 1945, when
one medium cargo ship and one small-medium
cargo ship were sunk, a medium cargo ship
was probably sunk and one escort vessel
was damaged.

Participated with credit as member of crew
USS TAUSSIG which was in Task Group 38.1,
part of Vice Admiral McCain's Task Force
38 under Admiral Halsey, Commander THIRD
Fleet, during the following air strikes
on Japanese Empire:

10,17,18,30 July 1945 — Tokyo Area
5,13,15 August 1945 — Tokyo Area
12,14,15 July 1945 — Northern Honshu
                    and Hokkaido.
24,25 July 1945 — Kure
9,10 August 1945 — Northern Honshu

         W. H. McClain
        W. H. MC CLAIN
        Commander, U.S. Navy
        Commanding

SUMMARY OF SERVICE

Vessel or Station	From—	To—	Rate
NTS NOB Norfolk, Va.	9 February 1939	15 April 1939	AS
U.S.S. MOFFETT (362)	27 April 1939	5 February 1941	AS,S2c,S1c,F2c
U.S.S. MELVILLE	5 February 1941	7 February 1941	F2c
U.S.S. MOFFETT (DD362)	7 February 1941	23 October 1942	F2c,F1c
RecShip New York	24 October 1942	28 December 1942	F1c
RS NYd Philadelphia, Penn.	29 December 1942	18 January 1943	F1c,MM2c
USNH Philadelphia, Penn.	18 January 1943	28 January 1943	MM2c
RecSta Nyd Philadelphia, Penn.	28 January 1943	19 February 1943	MM2c
U.S.S. SARANAC (AO-74)	22 February 1943	31 January 1944	MM2c, MM1c
R/S Terminal Island, Calif.	31 January 1944	16 February 1944	MM1c
NTS NOB Norfolk, Virginia	8 March 1944	18 May 1944	MM1c
U.S.S. HAUSSEG (DD-746)	20 May 1944	20 August 1945	MM1c

Final average in all marks upon discharge ___3.86___

H. Le CLAIR, Comdr., USN.
Signature and rank of Commanding Officer

12

...M THE U. S. NAVAL SERVICE

1. SERIAL OR FILE NO. RANK AND CLASSIFICATION	(FIRST) (MIDDLE) 2. DATE AND CLASS FOR 4. PERMANENT ADDRESS FOR MAILING PURPOSES	3. PLACE OF SEPARATION

255 87 39 CAMPBELL, John Emerson
MM1c USN

Box 254 Rainille, W. Va.

3. PLACE OF SEPARATION: USNTSC, Shelton, Va.

5. CHARACTER OF SEPARATION: HONORABLE

7. ADDRESS FROM WHICH EMPLOYMENT WILL BE SOUGHT: Box 254 Rainille, W. Va.

8. RACE	9. SEX	10. MARITAL STATUS	11. U. S. CITIZEN (YES OR NO)	12. DATE AND PLACE OF BIRTH
White	M	Single	Yes	17 May 1918 Landisburg, W. Va.

13. REGISTERED	14. SELECTIVE SERVICE BOARD OF REGISTRATION	15. HOME ADDRESS AT, TIME OF ENTRY INTO SERVICE
YES ☒ NO Greenbrier Co. W. Va.		Danese, West Virginia

16. MEANS OF ENTRY INDICATE BY CHECK IN APPROPRIATE BOX
☒ ENLISTED ☐ INDUCTED ☐ COMMISSIONED

9 Feb. 1939

17. DATE OF ENTRY INTO ACTIVE SERVICE: 9 Feb. 1939

18. NET SERVICE (FOR PAY PURPOSES) YRS. MOS. DAYS: 6 8 2

19. PLACE OF ENTRY INTO ACTIVE SERVICE: Charleston, West Virginia.

20. QUALIFICATIONS, CERTIFICATES HELD, ETC.: See Rating Description Booklet for MM1c.

21. RATINGS HELD: A3, S2c, S1c, F2c, F1c, MM2c, MM1c

22. FOREIGN AND/OR SEA SERVICE WORLD WAR II: ☒ YES ☐ NO

23. SERVICE SCHOOLS COMPLETED: None

24. SERVICE (VESSELS AND STATIONS SERVED ON): NTS, NOB, NorVa: USS MOFFETT(562) U.S. MELVILLE: USS MOFFETT(DD362) USS SARATAC (AO 74) NTS, NOB, NorVa: USS TAUSSIG (DD 746)

IMPORTANT: IF PREMIUM IS NOT PAID WHEN DUE OR WITHIN THIRTY-ONE DAYS THEREAFTER INSURANCE WILL LAPSE. MAKE CHECKS OR MONEY ORDERS PAYABLE TO THE TREASURER OF THE U. S. AND FORWARD TO COLLECTOR'S SUBDIVISION, VETERANS ADMINISTRATION, WASHINGTON-25, D.C.

25. KIND OF INSURANCE	26. EFFECTIVE MONTH OF ALLOTMENT DISCONTINUANCE	27. MONTH NEXT PREMIUM DUE	28. AMOUNT OF PREMIUM DUE EACH MONTH	29. INTENTION OF VETERAN TO CONTINUE INSURANCE
N	Oct. 1945	Nov. 1945	8.94	Yes

30. TOTAL PAYMENT UPON DISCHARGE	31. TRAVEL OR MILEAGE ALLOWANCE INCLUDED IN TOTAL PAYMENT	32. MUSTERING OUT PAY	33. NAME OF DISBURSING OFFICER
$ 121.31	$ 23.40	$100	R.H. ADAMS, LT.(JG)(SC)USN

34. REMARKS

35. SIGNATURE (BY DIRECTION OF COMMANDING OFFICER):
L. J. Snyder

L.J. SNYDER, Lt.Comdr., USNR.

36. NAME AND ADDRESS OF LAST EMPLOYER	37. DATES OF LAST EMPLOYMENT	38. MAIN CIVILIAN OCCUPATION AND D. O. T. NO.
Student	FROM:	Student
	TO:	

39. JOB PREFERENCE (LIST TYPE, LOCALITY, AND GENERAL AREA)	40. PREFERENCE FOR ADDITIONAL TRAINING (TYPE OF TRAINING)
Undecided	None

41. NON-SERVICE EDUCATION (YEARS SUCCESSFULLY COMPLETED) GRAM.: H. S.: COLL.:	42. DEGREES	43. MAJOR COURSE OR FIELD	44. VOCATIONAL OR TRADE COURSES (NATURE AND LENGTH OF COURSE)
8 4 0	0	Academic	None

45. RIGHT INDEX FINGERPRINT	46. OFF DUTY EDUCATION COURSES COMPLETED
	None

47. DATE OF SEPARATION: 10/22/45

48. SIGNATURE OF PERSON BEING SEPARATED:
John E Campbell

156

Marriage Certificate

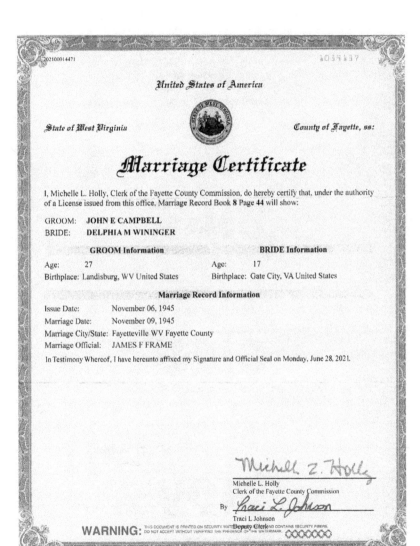

From the South Pacific to the New River family members

John Campbell was one of 13 children born in West Virginia, parents:

William Lee Campbell (descendants of George W. Campbell & Mary C. Hanshew) born: 8/11/1878 in Landisburg, WV

Died: 1/24/1958 in Beckley, WV

Nettie Priscilla Durham Campbell (descendants of Warren O. Durham & Angus Patience Halstead)

Born: 4/20/1885 in Campbells Creek, WV

Died: 10/27/1946 in Beckley, WV

Their children as follows:

Mary Patience Campbell — 5/23/1903 — 5/29/1993 — Married Dallas Hanshew — Married Frank "Rough" Hughes - 9/2/1941

William Adam "Add" Campbell — 9/24/1904 — 5/7/1978 — Married Grace Walker — 12/26/1928 divorced

Mabel Missouri Campbell — 4/9/1907 — 10/9/1978 — Married Tillmon Donald "Shorty" Simmons — 8/12/1940

David Clinton Campbell - 8/17/1909 - 3/8/1911

Macy Bell Campbell - 5/22/1911 - 2/8/2006 - Married Darrell Fisher - 11/20/1933

Mae "Hattie Campbell - 5/29/1913 - 11/12/1998 - Married John Kermit "Chuck" Parker - 2/12/1956

Ralph Wilson Campbell — 2/27/1915 — 3/6/1993 — Married Blanche Ozell Anderson 12/24/1934

Alfred Ray Campbell — 9/25/1916 — 11/9/1991 — Married Alreda Grace Arrington — 8/20/1940 — Married Elizabeth Alice Cottle - 1982

John Emerson Campbell — 5/17/1918 — 10/25/1988 — Married Delphia Mae Wininger — 11/9/1945

Leonard Robert "Cub" Campbell — 2/2/1920 — 3/9/1990 — Married Faye Frances Prater — 11/11/1950

Joseph Herbert "Herb" Campbell — 4/12/1922 — 12/22/1943

Mildred Jean "Jean" Campbell — 10/22/1923 — 11/30/2001 — Married Newman Settle — 7/30/1945

Kenneth Wade Campbell — 9/4/1925 — 6/18/2009 — Married Eileen Lucille Settle — 8/31/1951

These names have been mentioned as there is reference to some of these people in the letters referenced.

My father was a proud man and loved his home state of West Virginia. They were raised on a farm and as children we visited West Virginia (not his home site) on vacations and all of the people above that were still living were of a great impact on his and our lives, the ones that were no longer living also greatly impacted his life as we see in the letters also.

Delphia Mae Wininger Campbell

Parents — Kemp L. Wininger — born 1901 died 1949

Mary Claudia Price Wininger born 1/29/1910 — 6/6/1993 - Parents: Lawrence Price & Ida C Wygal

Siblings of Claudia — Edgar Price, Audrey Price Cottle, Imogene Price, Pauline Price Blake, June Price Johnson

Children of Kemp & Claudia Wininger

Delphia Mae Wininger — 8-12-1928 — 10/25/1998 — Born in Gate City, VA - Married John Emerson Campbell - 11/9/1945

Willard Larry Wininger - 7/26/1930 — 6/24/1985 — Born in WV — Married Marye Rice — 1959 - 1967

Married: Mary Catherine Welch - 1970 - 1985

Letter of Acknowledgement

This is to acknowledge those people that have been instrumental in these letters getting to the point that they are now.

Scott Emerson Campbell for his time in transcribing all of these letters to his daughter, Amy Campbell Darbyshire so that they are now preserved and able to be shared with the world as they are very unique, not different but special not only to the family of John & Delphia Campbell but to others also due to the conflict of WW11 and things mentioned in these letters.

A special thank you to the United States National Archives & Records Administration, for obtaining the military records of John & Herbert Campbell.

Gregg Campbell for his support along the way in doing this on behalf of our parents.

To all of the family and friends that have encouraged, given advice, and believed in putting these into book form. Please know that your encouragement means so much to the 3 of us.

Scott & Tracey

Printed in the USA
CPSIA information can be obtained
at www.ICGtesting.com
CBHW060735300923
1161CB00004B/6